DEVELOPMENT OF SELF-CONCEPT AND CAREER MATURITY

DEVELOPMENT OF SELF-CONCEPT AND CAREER MATURITY

Dr. Sharanjit Kaur

RAJAT PUBLICATIONS
New Delhi

Development of Self-Concept and Career Maturity
by *Dr. Sharanjit Kaur*

This edition is published by Rajat Publications
4740/23, Ansari Road Daryaganj,
New Delhi - 110002

ISBN: 978-81-7880-337-1

Edition 2026

Printed and bound in India

RAJAT
PUBLICATIONS

4740/23, Ansari Road, Daryaganj,
New Delhi- 110002 (India)
Mob:- +91-9811484973, +91-9811105389
E-mail: rajat_publication@yahoo.com

PREFACE

This book is one outcome of a research study conducted in New Delhi, under the able guidance of Prof. P. Gupta UGC, National Fellow, Lucknow University and Prof. J.S. Gaur, Ex-Head DEPC & G, NCERT, New Delhi.

A type of career plays an important role in ones life. An individual gives almost 10-12 hours in a day to his/her career. It is very important for an individual to be very careful. While making plans for career, especially in the 21 st century, where competition is very tough. The role of career counsellor has become very important.

In this book, I have described how personality variables such as self-concept and locus of control affect career maturity. A career counsellor should study these variables of an individual, while doing career counselling.

I wish to thank the many persons involved in the research study and in the development of the book: My teachers, parents and other members of the family, principals and students of participating schools.

The author is also thankful, to M/s Rajat Publications, New Delhi, who readily agreed to publish this book.

-Dr. S.J. Kaur

CONTENTS

1
INTRODUCTION

Work is the way of life. What type of life an individual leads will depend upon his or her occupation in which he or she is engaged. So, choosing an appropriate occupation is very important. There are many crucial factors, which influence while making a plan about future, career maturity is one of them. Career maturity is a concept related with career development. Career development is conceived as one of the important aspect of individual development. Career development is a process experienced over a period of them. In other words career maturity is nothing but the degree of career development.

The studies in the area of career development suggest that career maturity and vocational maturity as well as career development and vocational development are the synonym for each other. Career maturity and career development are only a new terminology for the old concepts.

The concept of vocational maturity can be traced to the work of Carter (1940) and Strong (1943). Carter studied the development of interests in adolescence, whereas Strong (1943) investigated interest maturity, and suggested that vocational behaviour changes systematically with age.

Dysinger (1950) appears to be the first person to

use the term 'vocational maturity' for depicting the development from immaturity to maturity in vocational planning. However, Super was the first person who worked systematically on vocational maturity.

Bartlett (1971), after reviewing the literature in relation to vocational maturity, found two different conceptualizations in defining and measuring vocational maturity: (i) the absolute or relative approach favoured by Super (1955) and Gribbons and Lohnes (1968), and (ii) the degree and rate approach advocated by Crites (1961) and Westbrook (1972). The main difference between these two conceptualizations is that the absolute or relative approach is couched in terms of stages of development and the mastery of tasks associated with them, while the degree and rate approach uses an individuals own peers as a comparison group.

Index of Vocational Maturity

The absolute index of vocational maturity is defined as: "The Life stage in which the individual actually is, as evidenced by the developmental tasks, with which he is dealing in relation to the life stage in which he is expected, to, in terms of his age" (Super and Overstreet, 1960).

The relative index of vocational maturity is an individuals' vocational behaviour maturity. "In the actual life stage (regardless of whether it is expected life stage), as evidenced by the behaviour shown in dealing with developmental tasks of the actual life stage compared with the behaviour of other individuals who are dealing with the some developmental tasks" (Super and Overstreet, 1960).

Crites (1961) described career maturity, as "the maturity of an individuals vocational behaviour as indicated by the similarity between his behaviour and that of the oldest individuals in his vocational life stages."

Crites (1961) described rate of vocational development as: "The maturity of an individual's vocational behaviour in comparison with that of his own groups."

The definitions described above had led to various methods and means of measuring and assessing vocational maturity. Super tended to investigate the construct and predictive validity of his definition. Crites' work has focused on the exploration of objective measurement of the group factor, vocational choice attitudes and competencies. Empirically, career maturity is defined as the rate and level of an individuals development.

Basic Concepts

The technical terms used in the present study can be explained as follows:

Self-concept: The concept by which an individual perceives himself/herself as a person with respect to his/her immediate environment. "The self-concept is the individual's way of looking at himself. It also signifies his way of thinking, feeling and behaving" (Saraswat and Gaur, 1981).

Locus of Control: A general term in social psychology, referring to the perceived source of control over one's behaviour. It is measured along a dimension running from high internal to high external, with an internal person being one who tends to take responsibility for his own actions and who views himself as having control over his own "destiny" and an external as one who tends to see control as residing elsewhere and attribute success and failure to outside forces.

Sex: "Sex is the sum of the structural, functional and behavioural peculiarities of living beings" (Websters Dictionary).

Career Maturity

Career maturity is the readiness to make appropriate career decisions (Lundberg et al. 1997).

Career maturity is manifested by behavioural and developmental tasks. This concept requires first to determine an individuals developmental task and life stage from his/her chronological age, and second, to identify his/her degree of vocational development within his/her life stage from his/her behaviours. For instance, for a 15 year old student, the expected life stage is the exploratory period of adolescence and the primary task of vocational development is the choice of an occupation.

Dimensions of Career Maturity

If vocational development is a continuum, and vocational maturity a point on this continuum, denoting degree of development attained, it becomes important to specify the dimension along which vocational development takes place, and on which vocational maturity is measured.

In order to measure vocational maturity, Super (1955) identified five major dimensions of vocational maturity during adolescence.

(i) ***Orientation of Vocational Choice:*** It means that one who is concerned with making choices is more likely to be ready and able to choose vocation, when called upon to do so than is one who is not concerned with choice.

(ii) ***Information and Planning:*** An individual should have collected some information about his preferred occupation for example, if she wants to be a doctor, then in order to obtain appropriate basic education and preliminary experience information about the preferred occupation (doctor) should take into account such factors as: (a) requirements including training and physical, mental and economic requirements; (b) duties, such as what is done, how it is done and what tools are used; (c) conditions of work, including monetary rewards, physical, psychic conditions, associated hours, seasonal and

cyclical regularity, security etc.; and (d) opportunities, including location, means of entry, lines of advancement and economic trends.

(iii) ***Consistency of Vocational Preferences:*** It is an important dimension of vocational maturity because greater maturity should result in a narrowing of goals, in the elimination of the less attractive preferences and in the crystallization of preferences which have stood the test of exploration and trail consistency may be indicated by the naming of only one occupation as the preferred vocation by the naming of more than one occupation as preferred while remaining consistent as to the preferred field of work, by, choosing occupations which require the same general level of ability or education, or by naming preferences which belong to the same field and level, and consistency of preferences over time.

(iv) ***Crystallization of Traits:*** It is another important dimension of vocational maturity on the grounds that the more highly developed and integrated the individual's ability and trait system the greater his readiness to cope with the developmental tasks of vocational choice and adjustment.

(v) ***Wisdom of Vocational Preferences:*** It has been viewed as one of the most complex, but at the same time conceptually most satisfying dimension of vocational maturity. This is because the other dimensions are unlikely to lead to vocational adjustment unless the resulting or inherent vocational preferences are wise. Wisdom of vocational preferences may be assessed by considering various indices such as the relationship between his abilities and preferences, the relationship between his measured interests and preferences, and the socio-economic accessibility of his preferred occupation.

Theories of Career Development

In a field that began as late as the early 1950, there is understandably a diversity of duplicating or supporting theories and of conflicting theories. These may be classified as follow:

(i) Trait and Factor Theory

This is one of the oldest theoretical approaches, which, assume that a straightforward matching of an individual's abilities and interests with the world's vocational opportunities can be accomplished and once accomplished, solves the problems of vocational choice for that individual. Some of the original trait factor theorists who influenced thinking about vocational psychology are Parsons (1909), Hull (1928) and Kitson (1925). The logic of this view point is that because individuals differ in their aptitudes, interests and personalities and because occupations requires varying amounts and kinds of these traits and factors, different individuals choose to enter different occupations. Parsons (1909) an early exponent of this view, explicated a three step process through which a person goes in choosing a vocation: (a) a clear understanding of his/ her aptitudes, abilities, interests, ambitions, resources, limitation and their causes; (b) a knowledge of the requirements and conditions of success, advantages and disadvantages, compensation, opportunities and prospects in different lines of work; and (c) true reasoning on the relations of these two groups of facts.

Certain objections have been raised by critics against the use of trait theory. Firstly the term trait is ambiguous. Under the same trait name individual give their own definitions e.g. sociability may mean tendency to seek company, interest in company etc., or it may mean tendency to get along with others, share feelings etc.

Secondly forms of behaviour assumed under any generalized trait may vary in a quantitatively definable manner along more than one dimension.

Thirdly, the question is raised whether it is really meaningful to describe the individuals in terms of traits they all have in common. On the one hand uniqueness of an individual, according to trait theory, is only a matter of quantitative difference from others; on the other hand, while we measure a trait we are looking for some behaviour of aspect of individual peculiar to him.

However, trait theory has found its application in psychological measurement much more than any other approach. Even now, few practitioners of vocational counselling are pure trait factor adherents.

(ii) The Situational Approach

This approach has as its central point the notion that societal circumstances beyond the control of the individual contribute significantly to career choices and that the principal task confronting a person is the development of techniques to cope effectively with the environment. Many investigators did studies and found that chance (Salamone and Slaney, 1981); social and ethnic background factors (Hollingshead's, 1949; social class membership (Lipsett, 1962, Sewell and Shah, 1968) affect the career choice of an individual.

(iii) Developmental/Self-concept Theory

This approach weaves two models into one and can be called either the developmental or the self-concept theory. The approach holds as its central theses that (a) individuals develop more clearly defined self-concepts as they grow older, although these vary to conform with the changes in one's view of reality as correlated with aging; (b) people develop images of the occupational world which they compare with their self-image in trying to make career decisions; (c) the adequacy of the eventual career decision is based on the similarity between an individual's self-concept and the vocational concept of the career eventually chosen.

This approach had its origin in the work of Buehler (1933), Lazarasfield (1931) and Center's (1940) work on interest pattern. The theory of Ginzberg et al. (1951) is also based on the developmental nature of vocational choice. Developmental theorist proposes that the decision involve in the selection of an occupation are made at a number of different points in the individuals life and that they constitute a continuous process which starts in childhood and ends in adulthood.

Ginzberg, Ginsburg Axelard and Herma (1951) constructed vocational choice as an irreversible process occurring in reasonably clearly marked periods and characterized by a series of compromises the individual makes between wishes and possibilities.

Donald Super's (1957) theory is based on ten propositions which reflects his use of trait and factor approach, his application of self theory and his interpretation of choice as a developmental phenomenon. He places even more emphasis than Ginzberg upon vocational choice as process. He introduced the concept of vocational maturity to denote the individual degree of development from the time of his early fantasy choices to his decisions about retirement from work in old age (Super, 1955).

The most systematic application of self-concept theory to vocational choice came in the career pattern study by Super and associates (1960, 1963). He proposes the notion that people strive to implement their self -concept by choosing to enter the occupation seen as most likely to permit self-expression.

1 fashioning his theory of career development, Donald Super appears to have been under two strong influences. The first influence, self-concept theory, may be illustrated by the writings of Carl Rogers (1942; 1951). Carter (1940), and Bordin (1943). These writers have suggested that behaviour is a reflection of an individual's attempt to implement his self-descriptive and self-evaluative though. With particular

preference to vocations. Bordin (1943) proposed the notion that responses to vocational-interest inventories represent an individual's projection of self-concept in terms of stereotypes held about occupations. A person selects or rejects an occupation because of the belief that the field is or in not consistent with a self-view.

The other major influence on Super's work is Charlotte Buehler's (1933). She suggested that life can be viewed as consisting of distinct stages. The first is a growth stage, starting at birth and ending around age 14. Following this is an exploratory stage, occurring between age 15 and 25. The maintenance stage comes next and covers the next 40 years, ending at about age 65, whereupon the final stage, called decline, beings. According to Buehler life takes vary according to the stage. Super's conception of career development is built upon the framework of these life stages and based on the assumption that vocational tasks reflect larger life tasks.

Super thought the Ginzberg work had serious shortcomings, one of which was the failure to take into account the very significant existing body of information about educational and vocational development.

Super's theoretical writings have been extensive. His initial formulations were stated in an address before the American Psychological Association (1953) and further elaborated in a book (1957), a monograph (Super et al., 1957) and several papers (most significantly 1963a, 1963b, and 1963c). Super proposes the notion that people strive to implement their self-concept by choosing to enter the occupation seen as most likely to permit self-expression. Furthermore, Super suggests that the particular behaviours a person engages in to implement the self-concept vocationally are a function of the individual's stage of life development. As one matures, the self-concept becomes stable. The manner is which it is implemented vocationally, however, is dependent upon conditions external to the individual. Thus, attempts to make vocational decisions during adolescence assume a different from that those made during late middle age. According to Super, diverse vocational behaviours can be understood better by viewing them within the context of the changing demands of the life cycle on the shape of attempts to implement a self-concept.

In the development of his theory, Super strived to implement a specific stream of thought and research in psychology. The attempt to build a theory on the groundwork laid by previous efforts was deliberate, since Super soundly criticized the Ginzberg theory because of the failure of its authors to use the existing data relevant to vocational choice.

Important to Super's theory is the difference between the psychology of occupations and the psychology of careers. The psychology of occupations is based primary on differential psychology and on the assumption that once on individual and career and matched they will "live happily ever after." On the other hand, the psychology of careers, stemming from developmental psychology, rests on the assumption that career development conforms to the general principles of human development, which are functionally evolutionary in nature. Vocational psychology is the term Super chose to represent the field of study resulting from the fusion of the two streams of thought. Since the methods and tools of vocational counselling are currently more suitable to the study of the psychology of occupations than the psychology of careers, Super asserts that the latter has been neglected in favour of the former (Super, 1961a; 1964a). He would correct the neglected condition of the psychology of careers by means of his theoretical formulations.

Super's theoretical framework is based on three psychological areas. The first is the field of differential psychology. The research related to differential psychology has reached maturity and has contributed much to vocational psychology. On the basis of existing data, Super drew the assumption that any given person possesses the potential for success and satisfaction in a variety of occupational settings. He elaborated on the trait-factor notions that people are differentially qualified for occupations by suggesting that interests and abilities are likely to fall into patterns more consistent with some occupations than others and that people are likely to be more satisfied if they are in an occupation that requires a pattern of interests and abilities closely corresponding to their own characteristics.

The second psychological influence on Super's theory stems form self-concept theory. Super proposed that vocational self-concepts develop on the basis of children's observations of and identifications with adults involved in work. The third influence is the principles of developmental psychology. The concept of life stages suggested by Buchler (1933) led Super to proposed that a person's mode of adjustment at one period of life is likely to be predictive of techniques use to adjust at a later period.

Developmental concept also led Super to the idea of career patterns. From the work of Miller and Form (1951) and Davidson and Anderson (1937), Super expanded the concept of career patterns. The career behaviour of people follows general patterns which may be recognized as regular and predictable after study and examination fo the individual. These patterns are the result of many psychological, physical, situational and societal factors which, when accumulated, make up an individual's life. Among the various career pattern are the *stable pattern,* in which a career such as *medicine* is entered into relatively early and permanently, the conventional pattern, in which several jobs are tried, one of which leads to a stable job; the *unstable* pattern, characterized by a series of trial jobs which lead to a temporary stability which is soon disrupted; and finally the *multiple trial* pattern, in which an individual moves from one stable entry-level job to another and which may be observed in domestic service careers (Super and others, 1957).

Super and several of his students published a series of papers which provided a more explicit and detailed set of statements about how vocational development occurs. Super began by making the notion of the self (as differentiated from the nonself) which an infant possesses at birth, Super described a process which leads first to primary self-percepts and then to more elaborate, or secondary percepts. The primary self-percepts deal with raw sensations such as hunger, pain and temperature. *As* the child matures and begins to develop secondary percepts, the sensations begin to become ordered and assume a relationship with one another. As maturation continues, the self-percepts become even more complex and abstract, developing into self-concepts and systems of self-concepts. Among the many system of self-concepts is the vocational self-concept, the system of major concern to Super.

According to Super (1963a), self-concept formation requires a person to recognize himself as a distinctive individual, yet at the same time to be aware of the similarities between himself and others. The self-concept of a well integrated individual is a continually developing entity, shifting somewhat through life as experiences indicate that changes are necessary to reflect reality. Presumably, the vocational self-concept develops in a similar way. As an individual matures, he tests himself in many ways, most of which have implications for educational and vocational decisions. The process begins with the self-differentiation that occurs as part of a person's search for identity, a child learns that touching a hot stove hurts. In adolescence, the differences between self and others are broadened and one becomes aware of being fat or tall, shy or poised, athletic or clumsy, good or bad in academic matters. These recognition's, in turn, lead to decisions about education and work that are consistent with self-concepts.

At the same time that the process of differentiation of self from others is occurring, a process of identification goes on, partly facilitating the differentiation and partly facilitated by it. Beginning with their identification with the like-sexed parent, children develop images of themselves and behaviour appropriate to culture gender-role stereotypes.

They progress from identification with general models to identification with specific models. Recognizing that his father's life is not ideal the adolescence male may find other adult males with whom to identify. The Grocer's son may model himself vocationally after the neighbour who is an engineer, while at the same time identifying with his father's hobbies and personality traits. Similarly, the young female searches for attractive female role models. If her mother is not an attractive model, the young woman will seek others.

Role playing, stimulated by the process of identification, further facilitates the development of the vocational self-concept. The youth who observes a firefighter will pretend to be one and will play games in which the role of fireman is acted. Growing older, the role playing becomes more subtle and sophisticated. The budding physician imagines performing great surgery and observes doctors in order to adopt their mannerisms and values.

Hadley and Levy (1962) have suggested that much of the role playing that occurs to facilitate career development takes place in formal and informal groups. The child evaluates potential roles in the world of work, from the point of view of the family, which communicates differential values toward various kinds of work. As the child reaches adolescence, the reference group shifts from the family to the peer group, and vocational role activities, real and vicarious, are evaluated in the context of the teenage world. In later life, when careers have been embarked upon and established, professional associations and trade unions serve as vocational reference groups. Code of conduct, modes of behaviour, and value are informally or formally set by the vocational group to which a person belongs.

In extension of his theory, Super (1993a) elaborated upon the concept of vocational maturity (Super et al., 1957, 1960). Vocational maturity allows the observer to assess the rate and level of an individual's development with respect to career matters. It is to be expected that vocationally mature behaviour will assume different shapes depending upon the context provided by an individual's life stage. The vocationally mature fourteen-year old will be concerned with assessing personal interests and abilities to reach the goal of deciding on an educational plan. While the vocationally nature forty-five year old person will be concerned with ways to maintain career status in the face of competition from younger workers.

To specify further the process of vocational development, Super (1963c) extended the analysis of life stages with reference to vocational behaviour. He proposed the idea that each of the two major stages in the vocationally significant life periods have several substages. The exploratory stage is composed first of the tentative substage, then the transition substage and finally the uncommitted trial substage. Following these periods is the establishment stage. Which is composed of the committed trial substage and the advancement substage. These stages, while not precisely the same as those of the Ginzberg theory starting in late childhood in tentative probes and questions, becoming stronger stirrings in early adolescence as recognition of the importance of these decisions grows, and finally leading to educational, and sometimes preliminary, vocational decisions. These decisions, in turn, are evaluated, are either modified or crystallized, and lead to the mature stage of elaboration and embellishment of vocational behaviours.

The process occurs by means of five activities when Super has called vocational development tasks. The first of these tasks, crystallization of a vocational preference, requires the individual to formulate ideas about work appropriate for himself or herself. It also requires development of occupational and self-concepts that will help mediate the individual's tentative vocational choice by means of relevant educational decision. While the crystallization task can occur at any age, as can all the vocational developmental tasks, it most typically occurs during the 14 to 18 year age range. Behaviours involve the awareness, use, differentiation, formulation and planning of concepts to use in determining actions regarding goals, interests and values, and occupations and preferences for each of the four stages; crystallization (14 to 18) specification (18-21), implementation (21-24), and stabilization (25-35).

The next vocational developmental task is the specifications of vocational preference. Here, the individual is required to narrow a general carrier direction into a specific one and take the necessary steps to implement the decision. Thus, the prospective applied physicist enrolls in an electrical engineering programme in college, while the student who likes the outdoors and has a technical bent beings the study of forestry. The specification task is most prominent during the 18-21 year age range. Once again, Super has indicated the attitudes and behaviours that are necessary to the successful accomplishment to the specification vocational task. They are similar to behaviours required in the crystallization task, except that they relate to the need for specification rather than crystallization. The third vocational task is the implementation of a vocational preference. This task, well advanced by age 21 and usually complete by age 25, requires the individual to complete some training and enter relevant employment, The necessary attitudes and behaviours of this task call for the individual's recognition of the need to plan for the implementation of a preference and the execution of this plan.

Stabilization within a vocation comes forth in the list of developmental tasks for career development. Occurring approximately between the age of 25 and 35, this task is represented by behaviour which reflect setting down within a field of work and the use of one's talents in use a way as to demonstrate the appropriateness of the career decisions previously made. It is to be expected that an individual changes *positions* during the stabilization period but rarely changes *Vocation*. The final vocational development task Super mentions is the consolidation of status and advancement, which occurs most clearly during the late 30s and mid 40s. Here the worker becomes firmly established, developing skills and seniority to achieve a secure and comfortable vocational position. The necessary attitudes and behaviours are highly similar to those of the implementation and stabilization tasks. While Super fails of mention the specific task of readiness for retirement and decline in his list of vocational tasks, he has called attention to this task as a final phase in the life cycle in other writings (Super, 1957).

In summary, the individual moves through life stages, each of which calls for vocational behaviours of a different sort. The adolescent is cast in the role of explorer searching for career direction. The young adult must translate the direction taken into action through training and job seeking. The more mature adult must find a place within a vocation, elaborate upon it, and secure a position. During each of these phases of vocational development, certain behaviours are more apt to result in growth than other. The degree to which the individual accomplishes the vocational tasks is a function of the adequacy with which the behaviours appropriate to each phase of development have been performed.

Following Ginzberg and Super emphasis upon vocational choice as a process which proceeds through several stages. Tiedman (1961); Tiedman and O'Hara (1965) have attempted to clarify and specify the series of decisions an individual makes in the course of his career development. He divides the overall process of vocational decision making into two periods, and then continues delineating stages with each period. First there is a period of anticipation which has four sub-stages: exploration, crystallization, choice and classification, and secondly there is a period of implementation and adjustment, which follows the classification stage of the anticipation period and which encompasses three additional stages, namely induction, reformation and incubation.

Tiedman and O'Hara (1963) also view career development as a function of the developing self. According to them self and vocational development interact and affect each other as the individual copes with problem of pursuing a course of training or deciding upon a career.

(iv) Personality Theories

This approach can be divided into two parts:

(i) Psychoanalytic conceptions of career choice;
(ii) Need theories.

Psychoanalytic Conceptions of Career Choice

According to Erik Erikson (1950), Freud once stated that the most significant indication of a psychologically normal being was the ability "to love and to work" effectively. Elaboration upon the first half of the statement, love, is not relevant here. The second aspect, however, illustrates the implicit role that work has in the psychoanalytic conception of personality and psychopathology. Basic is the system of psychoanalysis is the mechanism of sublimation. It provides an acceptable way for individual to release parts of his or her psychic energies that would be unacceptable in society if expressed directly. Work is ideally suited to provide outlets for sublimated wishes and impulses.

Several analytic writers have indicated that they are concerned, at least indirectly, with matters of vocational choice. Perhaps Brill of all the analysts devoted the most attention to career choice. He elaborated upon the notion that vocational section is one realm of behaviour in which society permits an individual to combine the pleasure and reality principles (1949). The pleasure principle drives an individual to behave in a manner that is immediately gratifying ignoring the future consequences of actions, while the reality principle focuses attention on eventual and long-term gratification's at the expense of immediate ones. In choosing a vocation an individual presumably is able to compromise between the two principles. Ideally, a person gets some immediate satisfaction as a consequence of the choice, while at the same time laying the foundation for future success. For example, the section of law as a career goal provides the law student with some prestige, status, and vicarious satisfaction in addition to the potential stability of eventual entry into the profession.

Brill further elaborated on the theme that sublimation is intimately bond up in vocational choice. He proposed that the particular vacation an individual chooses is vocational choice. He proposed that the particular vocation an individual chooses is not the result of an accidental arrangement of events. Rather, personality and impulses lead one to choose a career in which basic life impulses may be satisfied through sublimation. According to Brill, unconscious motives underlie all behaviour, including vocational selection. Brill documents his position by reporting several cases in which he personally observed the role that occupation plays in the gratification of impulses. To illustrate the role of psychopathological tendencies in career selection, Brill suggests that sadistic impulses may be satisfied in such diverse activities as those of butchers, surgeons and murders. Jones (1923) describes a patient who successfully transformed his childhood fascination with the process of urination and with bodies of water in general into a successful career as an engineer constructing bridges and canals. Zilboorg (1934) discusses a patient whose father, a successful toilet fixtures businessman, was extremely concerned with his son's bowel functions.

Brill concluded that physical and mental abilities alone play only a partial role in the kind of career a chooses" since sublimation is the key ingredient. While not taking a extreme a position as Brill, other psychoanalytic writers have illustrated how psychopathology, viewed in psychoanalytic terms, may account for vocational problems. By the case method, Bill (1960) illustrates the manner in which irrational vocational choices may persist in the service of ego integrity. Forer (1953), in depicting the role that personality variables play in vocational section, chose to stress the importance unconscious motivation has in the selection of career in relation to libidinal needs. Drasgow (1957) reported the results of a survey involving the reasons people had for selecting the vocation they chose. His results indicated that nearly every person in his very large sample expressed more than one reason for their choice. Such findings, he concludes, suggest that Freud's principle of over determination operates in vocational choice in that on one factor alone influences a career decision. It is the interaction of many factors.

Writing from the point of view that the pleasure and reality principles are not sufficient to account for much of human behaviour. Hendrick (1943) proposed a "work principle." In contrast to the behaviours derived from the reality principle, presumably based on libidinal energy, those dependent on the work principle are based on the instinct to master one's environment. The "mastery instinct" in its turn has a biological foundation which is a function of one's attempt to control or change some portion of the environment through the combined use of intellectual and neurological processes.

Need Theories

Whereas psychoanalytic explanations of vocational choice focus upon the defense mechanisms of the individual in the selection of an occupation, 'need theories' of choice give primary attention to the desires and wants which stimulate the individual to prefer one occupation to another. Driven by conscious and unconscious needs, individual seeks a vocation which will permit him to satisfy some of his basic needs.

The concept of the psychological need has a long and

distinguished history in psychology. Perhaps the most complex characterization of the operation of need has been presented by Henery Murray (1938) Murray proposed and extensive list of psychological needs involved in a wide variety of human functioning. These needs, in combination with environmental "press," permit the construction of hypotheses to explain individual behaviour Individuals are motivated to behave because of tension states. These may be reduced by needed satisfaction. In time, the organism is assumed to associate tension reduction with particular objects and behaviours. When certain recognizable tensions are perceived, the individual knows because of these associations what behaviour will reduce the tension and satisfy the motivating need. Thus, tension reduction comes under individual control through the identification of needs and relevant behaviour. One group of investigators applied Murray's thinking to the study of motivation for a career in teaching (Stem, Masing, Denoton, Henderson, and Levin, 1960).

A psychological needs conception, along with the idea of tension reduction through needs satisfaction, is in many ways ideally suited to explain numerous aspects of career section and maintenance. Thus, it is not surpassing that some years ago Darley and Hagendah (1955), reviewing the research concerning the relationships between vocational interests, occupational preferences and selections, and personality characteristics, concluded that interest patterns represent the various ways that individuals see of potentially meeting their personal needs in careers.

Hoppock (1957) expanded the needs approach to career development. He suggested a theory of occupational choice that was based mainly on the use of occupational information built upon personal needs. The rationale stemmed from the assumption that occupational activities are related to basic need and that the adequacy of occupation choice improves as people are better able to identify their own needs and the potential need satisfaction offered by a particular occupation. Thus, Hoppock reasoned that "satisfactions can result from a job which meet our needs today or from a job which promises to meet them in the future." According to the needs reduction approach to career development, a hungry person will take any job to obtain enough to eat. Once the need for food has been reduced, a new job which offers the potential of satisfying other physical and psychological needs will be sough. To the degree that one can find that enter jobs relevant to higher order needs the more or less satisfied with work one will be.

A number of studies have taken an approach which has explored the role that psychological needs play in determining occupational decision and membership. Suziedelis and Steimel (1963) compared inventoried needs measured by the Edwards Personal Preference Schedule with inventoried interests measured by the Strong Vocational Interest Blank, to test the hypothesis that certain needs are characteristically found to people who enter particular occupations. A sample of college freshmen and sophomores was tested with the EPPS and then subdivided so that for each of the Edwards needs a group of Ss earned high scores and another group low ones. The frequency of A and B+ scores on each of the SVIB occupational groups was tabulated for each group of subjects. These procedures allowed the identification of interest areas thaf are systematically related to the Edwards need.

Some of the resulting correlations are intuitively reasonable. For example, high interest scores is the biological and physical sciences and literary occupations might well be expected to related to achievement needs, as was indeed found to be the case. Order needs seemed to be negatively related to similarity of interest to those of men social service and literary occupations. Curious, however, is the failure to find a relationship between order needs and business detail interests and the low correlation between affiliation needs and similarity of interests to those of men in business contact occupations.

Through data such as those reported by Suziedelis and Steimel interesting little more is understood about personality and career as a result. The correlation between responses on two inventories seems to be too far removed from the real world of both personality and occupational interest to reflect meaningful behaviour. As best, the results must be subject to highly cautions interoperations.

In another study of a similar kind, Bohn (1966) related needs inferred from responses to an adjective checklist to Holland personality type was found to be high on abasement need and low on dominance and heterosexual needs. Other findings however, are .more in line with exception: conventional people were high on achievement, order, affiliation, dominance, and defensiveness needs, and Enterprising subjects were high on achievement, exhibition, affiliation dominance and heterosexual needs.

Blum (1961) predicated that a positive relationship between desires for security and choice of highly secure occupations would be found. Blum also examined the relationship between personality (defined in tepms of EPPS scores) and the background factors of Ss emphasizing security in their vocational choices. To accomplish these ends he administered the EPPS, a biographical information questionnaire, and a homemade security needs inventory to 513 Ss, which resulted in 346 usable protocols. Blum found that the Ss with the highest score on security desires close occupations involving a secure setting such as civil service jobs or teaching, while avoiding relatively unstable but high payoff careers such as law.

Some unusual finding occurred, however. For example, business careers were highly sought by the security seekers. Do these latter choices reflect attempts to gain the security of large organizational membership? Security desires were , significantly correlated with EPPS needs deference, order succorance, abasement, and nurturence and negatively related to needs achievement, autonomy, dominance, and change.

Dipboye and Anderson (1961) studied the relationship between occupational stereotypes and needs on the assumption that the stereotypes reflect, to some degree, projections of needs relevant to occupational membership. An instrument descriptive of fourteen needs based on EPPS items was devised and administered to male and female high school seniors with instructions to rate each of several occupations on the degree of the accuracy of the description. The resulting stereotypes reflected cultural estimates to the occupations. For example, scientists were . seen as having high needs for endurance, achievement, and change, while high school teachers were perceived as high on needs order and change, while high school teachers were perceived as high on needs order and intraception. Boys saw engineers as high on achievement and order needs and physicians as high on nurturance, intraception, and achievement needs. Girls perceived nurses as having high nurturance, intraception, order and endurance needs. The findings are suggestive about the nature of needs as related to occupational section and membership.

Hall and Nougaim (1968) have studied needs and career development in the context of organizational characteristics. Their observations led them to conclude that the needs individuals exhibit in connection with their careers are not unchanging. Over a five-year period, Hall and Nougaim found that as managers advance, their affiliation, achievement, seem, and self-actualization needs increase and their safety needs decrease (these results are consistent with Maslow's theory). In another study, Bradshaw (1970) found similar results for professional men. These results indicate, though tentatively, that opportunities for higher order needs satisfaction in work increase as one moves up the vocational hierarchy.

It seems reasonable to except, if one postulate needs as a factor in occupational selection, that needs satisfaction is directly related to job satisfaction. Schaffer (1953) devised a questionnaire designed to measure the strength of each of 12 needs, the degree to which each need is being satisfied in one's and overall job satisfaction and administered it to 113 subjects in various industries, department stores, and government agencies. Though the questionnaire was distributed through administrators in this agencies, participation was voluntary, and the questionnaire was completed during the subject's personal time. As a result, only 32 of the 113 questionnaires was completed and returned, raising serious questions about the generality for the findings. Generally, the strongest needs expressed were for creativity and challenge, followed by needs for mastery, achievement, and social welfare. The lowest needs were socioeconomic rewards and the expression of dependency. Examination of the correlation's between an individual's needs and the degree to which they are satisfied in his job revealed significant relationships for the three highest needs. More important, the correlation of 0.58 between the mean satisfaction of the subjects' two strongest needs in the job and overall job satisfaction was highly significant.

A study similar in objective was conducted by Walsh (1959). He tested the hypothesis that subjects like or dislike job duties which are consistent or inconsistent, respectively, with their needs. To test the hypothesis he devised a Job Description Questionnaire (JDQ) containing 24 job descriptions with 8 duties each to which Ss were to respond in terms of the appeal the duties had for them. In addition, the Ss, 96 college males in an introductory psychology course, took the EPPS and were asked to recommend two features of each job which should be emphasized and two which should be de-emphasized in a recruiting campaign. Correlations were then computed between the EPPS scores and the needs reflected in the duties the Ss selected to be emphasized or de-emphasized. Of the 24 correlation that were computed, 17 are significant, leading considerable support to Walsh's hypothesis.

Wolf (1970) has gone so far as to propose a "theory" of job motivation on the basis of the Harzberg, Mausner, and Snyderman (1959) and Maslow (1954) theories combined. According to Wolf, the level of need gratification as defined by Maslow is important to satisfaction-dissatisfaction, the *content* of the activity is involved in factors are not so involved.

Orpen and Pinshaw (1975) found result confirming the relationship of job satisfaction to perceived need fulfilment, based on the responses of 100 insurance clerks who were given Porter's Need Fulfilment Questionnaire, Halpern's job Satisfaction Scale, and a overall 7-point rating scale to measure job satisfaction.

Probably, the most prominent need theory of vocational choice is the one formulated by Anne Roe (1956, 1957). In her theory Roe (1957) traces the effects of early psycho-social experiences on the formation of needs and patterning of psychic energy.

The ways in which the parents satisfy the needs of their children have an effect upon the factors which will determine an individual's, vocational behaviour. Those needs which parents fulfil routinely as they appear, have little affect upon the factors which determine an individual's, vocational behaviour, but needs which they satisfy only minimally or with delay become unconscious motivators - and directly influence the individual's preferences for activities, which involve working with things or with people, and which are the basis for vocational choice. The specific needs which Roe related to vocational choice, are those defined by Maslow (1954) in his theory of personality. Maslow has given a hierarchy of needs , the higher order needs only become effective after the lower order needs have been satisfied, therefore it is the higher order needs which act as rriotivating for vocational behaviour. In particular, it is the need for self-actualization which is of paramount importance. Roe maintains that this need is central in the choice of vocation. Since, all that a man can be, he must be, if he is happy. Roe does not relate specific needs to specific occupations rather she points out, how any occupation may serve to satisfy needs at a given level.

(v) Holland's Career Typology Theory of Vocational Behaviour

Holland's conception of career development grew from his experiences with people involved in making career decisions. He observed that most people view the vocational world in terms of occupational stereotypes. Instead of concluding that such stereotypes. Instead of concluding that such stereotyping confuses people and causes vocational counsellors extra difficulty, Holland turned the stereotyping process to nis advantage by assuming that it is based on the individual's experience with work thus being based on reality and possessing a high degree of accuracy and utility.

Holland's work has been characterized by four attributes: change, simplicity, instrumentation, and data. These environments are the realistic (for example, farmers, and truck drivers), the investigative (chemists, biologists), the'social (social workers, teachers), the conventional (bookkeepers, bank tellers), the enterprising (salesmen, politicians), and the artistic (musicians, artists).

The developmental hierarchy is represented by the individual's adjustment to the six occupational environment. Every one is required to adjust to each of the environments and develop certain skills, which reference to the setting. The six types of adjustment stemming form the developmental hierarchy represents major life styles and patterns of relationships Between the individual and the world. The most typical way an individual responds to the environment, is of curse, the modal personal orientation. The six orientations were referred to by the same names as the occupational environments in earlier versions of the theory but were renamed by Holland Later (1962; 1971). In the following descriptions of the orientations, the original names are the parentheses.

The *Realistic* (Motoric) orientation is characterized by aggressive behaviour; interest in activities requiring motor coordination, skill and physical strength; and masculinity. People oriented toward this role prefer "acting out" problems; they avoid tasks involving interpersonal and verbal skills and seek concrete rather than abstract problem situations. They score high on traits such as concreteness, physical strength, and masculinity and low on social skill and sensitivity.

The *Investigative* (Intellectual) persons' main characteristics are thinking rather than acting, organizing and understanding rather than dominating or persuading and sociability rather than sociability. These people refer to avoid close interpersonal contact, though the quality of these avoidance seems different from that of their Realistic colleagues.

The *Social* (Supportive) people seem to satisfy their needs for attention in a teaching or therapeutic situation. In sharp contrast to the Investigative and Realistic people. Social people seek close interpersonal situation and are skilled in their interpersonal relation, while they avoid situations where they might be required to engage intellectual problem solving or use extensive physical skills.

The *Conventional (Conforming)* style is typified by a great concern for rules and regulations, great self-control, subordination of personal needs, and strong identification with power and status, this kind of person prefers structure and order and thus seeks interpersonal and work situations where structure is readily available.

The *Enterprising* (Persuasive) people are verbally skilled, but rather than use their verbal skills to support others as the Social types do, they use them for manipulating and dominating people. They are concerned about power and status as are the Conventional people, but differ in that they aspire to the power and status while the Conventional honour others for it.

The *Artistic* (Esthetic) orientation manifests strong self-expression and relations with other people indirectly through artistic expression. They dislike structure and prefer tasks emphasizing physical skills or interpersonal interactions. They are interceptive and asocial much like the Investigatives, but differ in that they are more feminine than masculine, show relatively little self-control and express emotion more readily than most people.

The development of the styles corresponds to the general notions of most theorists concerning personality development. Personality is seen as a result of genetic and environmental influence. Holland does, however, indicate the way in which these modal orientations influence vocational behaviour once the OI orientations have been clearly established. If one orientation is clearly dominant over the other, the individual will seek an occupational environment that corresponds to the orientation.

The "practical, hard-heated" person will thus choose to become an engineer while the aggressive, verbal, ambitions one will easily decide that law is the right *career*. If two or more orientations are the same or nearly the same in their strength, the individual will vacillate the selection of an occupational environment. A person characterized by detached thought about problems, avoidance of close interpersonal relations, and a tendency to organize, combined with desire to exert self-control and considerable desire to be emotionally expressive, may one day choose to be a biologist and the next day to be graphic artist. If environmental factors interfere with the implementation of the first clear-cut orientation, then the individual will seek an occupational environment appropriate to the second strongest orientation. A student blacked in attempts to implement an Investigative choice of oceanography because financial resources are not adequate might will select the field of mechanical engineering, representing the second major orientation, the Realistic. However, if the hierarchy of orientations is not well ordered beyond the first one, then vacillation into selection of an occupational environment will occur, just as if the first two orientations were not clearly different in their strength.

The modal orientation exerts a clear influence on the particular occupational environment an individual chooses and whether or not indecision is experienced. The question of the level within an occupational environment that the individual chooses in a function of several other variables, entitled the level hierarchy. The level hierarchy is defined in terms if the individual's intelligence and self-evaluations.

A very important concept that lias been used by many investigators to test aspects of Holland's theory has been the notion of congruence. Congruence is supposed to reflect the degree to which an individual's personal qualities match the environmental demands of the occupational area chosen. It is therefore relatively easy to assess the degree to which the individual matches up to the demands by comparing Vocational Preference Inventory Scores or Self-Directed Search Scores to the proper personality Scores demanded by each of the major occupational areas in a publication such as *The Job Finder,* Congruence is in fact, one of the principle dependent outcomes associated with Holland's theory.

In addition to the concept of self-evaluation, which it will be recalled, was one of the two critical variables contributing to the individual's level hierarchy. Holland introduced a concept known as *self-knowledge*. Self-knowledge refers to the amount and accuracy of information an individual has about him or herself. It differs form self-evaluation, which refers to the *worth* the individual attributes to him or herself. However, these two constructs are not clearly differentiated. They seem to be highly interdependent and might well refer to two parts of the same phenomenon. Holland apparently introduces these constructs separately to permit himself to predict the adequacy of vocational choice for people who have self-evaluations based closely on accurate self-knowledge, as opposed to those whose vocational choice are partially based on self-evaluations founded on inadequate self-knowledge.

Holland state that the adequacy of occupational choice is largely a function of the adequacy of self-knowledge and occupational knowledge. The great the amount and accuracy of he information the individual has about each, the more adequate is the choice.

Social-Learning Approach

Probably the only significant innovation of the 1970s in career development theory is the application of social learning theory to career decision making. Like other career development theories, social learning theory applied to career decision making attends primarily to identifying and explicating the personal and environmental events that shapes individuals' decisions about careers made at major choice points in life. There are mainly four points in this theory:

1. Concern with inherited attributes such as race gender and physical appearance and with special apparently inherited abilities involving motor, intellectual and perceptual behaviours.

2. Concern with environmental events and settings in which these events occur, dealing, for example, with the social climate, individual experience, the job market, the training options and opportunities available to the individual, the social policies which affect career decisions, such as selection procedures, labour laws, union rules and retirement policies.

3. Concern with learning histories. These are divided into two types, (a) Associative learning experiences are those in which the individual observes relationships between events and is able to predict contingencies, (b) Instrumental learning experiences are those in which the individual operates on the environment directly with observable outcomes.

4. The last ingredient is the task approach skills. These skills are the result of unspecified interactions among the inherited attributes, environmental events and the learning histories.

Out of the combination of inheritance, environment, learning histories and tasks approach skills three consequences are postulated and are considered to be very important. First are self-observation generalizations. These are self-views that the individual learns based on life experiences. A second major consequence is the task approach skills. There are characteristics cognitive and affective predisposition that the individual displays in dealing with, interpreting and predicting the environment. The final major consequence is the action outcomes. The outcomes are specific decision-related behaviours that grow out of self-observation, generalizations and the task approach skills. For example, these might include making specific job skills, seeing one's way through specific job training programmes and other activities.

In conclusion, one can say, that almost all theories presented above, view career choice as the result of a match between the person and the occupation. Trait and factor theory, for example, asserts that people seek out jobs with requirements that are consistent with their personality traits. Holland's theory sees people as choosing work environments that are congruent with their personality types. In contrast the theories of Roe stress intrinsic personality needs as the primary determinants of choice, while Super is concerned about the developmental stages that occur throughout the lite span.

Need of Studies on Career Maturity

1. High School is the last stage of general education in India, and students need to make vocational and academic choice at this time. An understanding of the students career maturity and providing appropriate education should be of concern.

2. Although career guidance is usually stressed in schools of India, only a few studies (Agarwal, 1981; Parlikar, 1973; Gupta, 1973) have been conducted in the field of career development. The information associated with career maturity of students is needed by school counsellors. Therefore, the knowledge of career maturity of students still needs to be clarified in India.

3. It has been found that career maturity is significantly related with success in vocational training (Cox, 1968), vocational adjustment (McNamara, 1975), and vocational satisfaction (Enderlein, 1975). It is necessary to understand the career maturity of students in order to design an effective career preparation programme.

4. Since the economic development of India has come to the industrialization stage, the occupational jobs will be more differentiated than ever. Career adjustment of the individuals will mostly depend on their understanding of the world of work and,, their appropriate choice of careers. The development of career programmes, based on the study of career maturity of students may help them to become well prepared workers in their careers.

2

TRENDS OF SELF-CONCEPT AND CAREER MATURITY

The purpose of the literature review is to expand upon the context and background of the study to further defining the problem and to provide an empirical basis for the subsequent development of hypotheses. Borg and Gall (1983) mention that the review can also help in reaching a number of specific goals, namely delimiting the research problems, seeking new approaches, avoiding sterile approaches.

Researches conducted in India and abroad have considered various aspects of career maturity, such as demographic (Sex, SES, Age, Race, Caste, etc.), family related (child rearing practices, family cohesiveness, etc.), personality pattern (self-concept, locus of control, self-monitoring, self-sufficiency, etc.).

The review of empirical studies related to (i) self-concept and career maturity; (ii) locus of control and career maturity; (iii) sex and career maturity have been presented as follows:

Self-concept as Related to Career Maturity

Employing the Career Maturity Inventory - Attitude Scale and Coopersmith Self-Esteem Inventory, Dillard

(1976) stated that there existed slight to low moderate relationships between vocational maturity and self-concept among suburban middle-, urban middle-, and urban lower-class black males. Jones, Hansen, and Putnam (1976) gave Vocational Development Inventory-Attitude Scale and Tennessee Self-Concept Scale to 8th and 12th grade students. Results indicated that there was significant relationship between vocational attitude maturity and self-concept. Mintzer, Rhoda Greenberg (1976) took a sample of 480 boys and girls from 7th, 9th and 12th grades. Results indicated that self-concept was a statistically significant, but weak predictor of vocational maturity, was a weak correlate. Using the Career Maturity Inventory-Attitude Scale and Tennessee Self-Concept Scale, Seaward (1977) indicated that there was a significant correlation between vocational maturity and self-concept among high school students.

Using the Vocational Development Inventory-Attitude Scale and Tennessee self-concept scale, Putman, Hosie, and Hansen (1978) reported that a significant relationship between self-concept and vocational maturity was found among 11th grade students. Ronald E. Pound (1978) administered Crite's Vocational Development Inventory Attitude Scale (1969) and Tennessee Self Concept Scale (Fitts, 1965) among 500 males and 500 females. It was found that there was a significant relationship between self-concept and career maturity. Lawrence George (1978) conducted a study on black male community college students. Super's theory was only partially supported in that the self-concept was found to be a moderate predictor for the cognitive measure (Information and decision making) of vocational maturity.

Brumlow, Sharon Lorraine (1980) gave Tennessee self-concept scale and crite's Career Maturity Inventory to High School students. A statistically significant relationship was found between these students' overall self-concept and their career attitude maturity. It was also observed that each component (physical, moral, ethical, personal, family and social self) was related to levels of career attitude maturity. McNair David (1981) conducted a study on 259 10th grade students and found that the best predictors of career maturity for male and female group was self-concept. Huntington, Meath, James, Stewart (1982) found significant correlation between self-concept and career maturity.

Nwachukwu, Uchenna Ignatius (1983) gave CDI (College and University form) and Tennesse self-concept scales to 160 subjects. Positive correlation was found between levels of career maturity and self-concept. Anderson, Gregory Robert (1983) administered Crites' Career Maturity Inventory (1973) among 48 students of 8th grade. Results indicated that self-concept was significantly related to self-appraisal (one of the scale of choice competencies) and choice attitudes. Okun, Nicole, L. (1984) found positive correlation between self-concept and career maturity.

Locus of Control as Related to Career Maturity

Ifenwanta, Samuel Sunday Mpama (1979) gave Rotter I-E Scale and Career Maturity Inventory (Crites, 1965) to 40 Nigerian College students. Significant correlation between locus of control and career maturity was supported by both the scale. Drake, Jeffrey, William (1979) administered Career Development Inventory (Crites, 1965) and Intellectual Achievement Responsibility Questionnaire (Crandall, Crandall & Katkovsky, 1965) among 320 Sophomores in four selected suburban high schools. Results indicated positive correlation between internal locus of control and career maturity.

Positive correlation between Locus of Control and Career Maturity was found among 69 business college women (Lowan, Grace Joely, 1979). Grossman, Betty Jane (1979) gave CMI, Competence Test (Crites, 1973) and Differential Situations Inventory (Gardner & Warren, 1977) to high school students. Post hoc correlation coefficients were computed to see the correlation between one measure of career maturity: career competence and locus of control. Positive correlation was found.

Curry, John Anthony (1980) found positive significant correlation between Locus of Control and Measures of Career Maturity. Similar results were found in other studies conducted by Mobley John Emory (1980), and Bigelow, Elizabeth A. (1981).

Dwyer, Kevin Michael (1981) administered Different situations Inventory, Self Report Form (Gardner & Warren, 1978), Crites' Career Maturity Inventory (Attitude and Competence Scale, 1973) Post-hoc analysis utilizing product moment co-efficient of correlation found positive significant correlation between locus of control and one measure of career maturity (Attitude Scale). Robinson, Levie Tycho (1981) conducted a study on 399 University students. It was found that internality on the I-E Scale was significant correlate of mature career attitudes. Doods, Betty, May (1983) found a weak positive correlation between career maturity (Crites, 1973) and children's Nowicki Strickland Locus of Control for LH students on self-procured job. Okum, Nicole, L. (1984) found positive correlation between career maturity and greater internality. Naidoo (1998) found that career maturity as influenced by locus of control.

(III) Sex as Related to Career Maturity

Barbara, A. Putman & James C. Hansen (1972) gave Crite's Vocational Development Inventory (1969) to XI grade students and found that girls tend to be somewhat vocationally immature in comparison with their male classmates. Crane, Beverly, Brown (1978) administered the Adult Vocational Maturity among 448 undergraduate students. Results indicated significant differences in career maturity on the basis of sex was revealed with college female being significantly more career mature than college males. Seik Daniel Russell (1978) gave the attitude scale and the competence test of the career maturity (Crites, 1973) to 10th, 11th and 12th grade students. It was found that females scored significantly higher on competence scale.

A significant difference between males and females in relations to career maturity was found in another study conducted by Ronald E. Pount (1978).

Lee, Jae Chang (1979) gave adult vocational maturity to 527 undergraduate students. Results indicated significant differences in the career maturity of university students on the basis of sex, with college females being significantly more career mature than college males. Drake, Jeffrey William (1979) found females scored higher than males on Career Development Inventory (Crites, 1969). Shield, Halcline (1979) gave Career Maturity Inventory (Crites, 1973), to 84, 11th and 12th grade students. Results indicated girls were more career mature than boys.

Riese, Narda, Joann (1980), administered career maturity Inventory-Attitude Scale, and four of the five components of the competence test (Crites, 1973), among 300 Caucasian students. It was found that sex was significant with regard to attitude scale. Perez, Carlos, Alberto (1980), gave Career Maturity Inventory (Crites, 1973) to 200, 9th and 12th grade students, sex differences were found to be significant in two out of three of the vocational maturity measures employed. Sex differences was found statistically significant with respect to Career-Attitude Maturity levels in another study conducted by Brumlow, Sharon Lorraine (1980).

Butler, Dennis, Arther (1981) gave five components of the Career Development Inventory - Form III - Career Planning, Career Exploration, Career Decision Making, world of work information and knowledge of preferred occupation to 559 students of Class VII, IX, XI and of community and business college. Results indicated that females were significantly more mature than males in the area of career planning, career decision making and world of work information. Burkhead, Emily Jane (1981) administered Career Maturity Inventory Attitude Scale and two subscales of Competence test, i.e. self-appraisal and problem solving among 40 physically disabled and 46 non-disabled undergraduate students. It was found that female college students, both disabled and non-disabled were more vocationally mature than male college students.

Utairat, Weerawat (1981) conducted a study on 900 students of 5th, 8th and 11th grade. Significant differences were found between male and female students at all three grade levels in relation to vocational maturity. McNair, David (1981) gave Career Maturity Inventory – Attitude Scale (Crites, 1973) to 259 students of 10th grade. It was found that sex had a significant effect on career maturity scores. In another study conducted by Smith Ranson (1981), it was found that correlation between sex and career maturity was too weak to be statistically significant.

Pernicano, Kewin, Michael (1982) conducted a study and found that women scored higher than men on all measures of Career Maturity Inventory (Crities, 1973). Nwachukwu, Uchenna Ignatius (1983) conducted a study by administering a Career Development Inventory (College and University Form) to 160 subjects. It was found that females were more mature than males in their decision making and have a greater knowledge of the world of work, Anderson, Gregory Robert (1983) administered Career Maturity Inventory (Crites, 1973) among 48 students of grade VIII . It was found that females were significantly higher on choice attitudes. In another study conducted by Yankowitz, Robert, Bruce (1983) found sex related differences on all measures of Crites' Career Maturity Inventory (1973).

Spurlock, Laverne, Beard (1984) conducted a study on black high school seniors. Attitude scale of Crites'

Career Maturity Inventory (1973) was given to them. Results indicated that the participants differed by sex in their levels of career maturity and sex was a significant predictor of their career maturity. In another study conducted by Donald, E. Super and Dorothy D. Nevil found that girls scored slightly higher than boys on Crites' Career Development Inventory. Donahue Joan Marie (1985) gave Crites' Career Maturity Inventory Attitude Scale (1973) to 60 boys and 78 girls. It was found that girls has higher career maturity scores than boys.

Cesarano-Delacruz, Carol (1986) conducted a study on 31 males and 56 female graduate students. Results indicated that males were found to have significantly higher career planning and career development attitude scores than females. In another study conducted by Stewart, Prudence Jean (1986) gave vocational development inventory to 293 adult students to ascertain the degree of vocational maturity. It was observed that males had lower mean scores than females in each of the four career development states. Booth, Janis, Grawford (1986) administered Crite's Career Maturity Inventory (1973), among 216 community college students. It was found that there were significant differences in career maturity scores for males and females.

Smith, Gerald Ernest (1987) gave Crites' Career Maturity Inventory - Attitude Scale (1973) to 234 students. In this study, females displayed significantly more career maturity than males. Rodebaugh, Helen, Davis (1987) conducted a study on XI grade students and found that females scores surpassed those of males on factors of career maturity. In another study conducted by Kenneth C. Windish (1987) found that mature attitudes towards career were higher for girls.

There were many other studies which found no relationship between sex and career maturity. Mintzer, Rhoda, Greenberg (1976) conducted a study on 480 boys and girls of 7th, 8th, 9th and 12th grades. Results indicated that sex was not a predictor of vocational maturity. Seik, Daniel, Russell (1978) found that there was no significant differences in the scores of 10th, 11th and 12th grades boys and girls on the attitude scale of Crite's Career Maturity Inventory (1973) Nimkuntod, Parnarai (1978) found no differences in mean CMI- Attitude scale scores between males and females. Prince, Nancy Ryan (1978) found no significant differences between males and females on the total scale of Career Development Inventory (1973).

Gergely, Anthony Francis (1979), conducted a study on 573 IX grade students and found no significant differences between males and females.

No Significant differences existed between males and females in relation to career maturity, in a study conducted by McCaffrey (1980). Riese, Narda, Joann (1980), conducted a study on 300 Caucasian students. It was found that sex was not significant with regard to the competence scores of Crite's Career Maturity Inventory (1973). Giammatteo, Robert. R. (1980) found no significant correlation between sex and vocational maturity. Sex did not appear to have meaningful influence on vocational maturity in another study conducted by Mohy, Yvonne, Cecilia (1980).

Mause Rarayanni (1981) conducted a study on 89 emotionally maladjusted and 92 well adjusted high school students. Results indicated no significant differences between male and females in relation to career maturity. Mar-Brennan, Carolina Del (1981) gave Crites' Career Maturity Inventory (1973) to 104 students. No significant differences were found for career maturity in relations to sex.

Huntington Meath, James Stewart (1982) conducted a study and found that there was no significant differences between boys and girls in relation to career maturity. Similar results was found in a study conducted by Carter Arthur Wesley (1982). Friedberg, Sharon Ann (1983) conducted a study and found that sex was not predictive of vocational maturity of high school students. Sex on the six scale of career maturity inventory found no significant differences in a study conducted by Isralsky, Marc (1983). Caston Roberta Elizabeth Parsons (1983) also found no significant differences between males and females in relation to career maturity.

Keefer, Roxanne Kay (1985) found no significant relationship between career attitude maturity and variable of sex. Floyd, Mary Emma Steadman (1985) found no mean differences between the male and female respondents in five of the six subscales. Piper, James, W. (1986) conducted a study on 1,080 students of 10th and 12th grades. No significant differences recorded between male and female career maturity scores. Kunnu, Felex, Bandele (1988) found that sex was not significant correlate of career maturity. Fouad Nadya A. (1988) Gave Crite's Career Maturity Inventory (1973) to 801 students of U.S. and 537 students of Israel. Results indicated no differences in career maturity scores for males and females.

Indian Studies Conducted on Career Maturity

Parlikar (1973) investigated the vocational maturity of High School Students. Kethuria (1974) probed into some personality determinants of vocational maturity and career indecisiveness. Hukum Chand (1979) conducted a study to find out the factors i.e. SES, rural-urban background, grade, academic achievement, self-concept, affecting career maturity of class VIII, IX and X of rural-urban students of Chandigarh.

Agarwal (1981) studied the relationship of career maturity with selected socio-psychological variables and to find out the most relevant variables which would predict career maturity at the three grade levels in boys as well as in girls.

Tulsi (1983) probed the effect of career guidance

strategies on vocational maturity patterns arising on account of differences in intelligence, sex and need achievement of students. Gaur et al. (1987) aimed at investigating psychological characteristics like self-concept, occupational aspiration, values, intelligence and career maturity against educational and vocational maturity of scheduled caste high school students.

The present study was concerned with the personality aspect of career development. Among many personality variables, two important personality characteristics i.e., self-concept and locus of control have been chosen for in-depth study. A demographic variable i.e. sex has also been taken to see the significant differences between boys and girls.

3

IDENTIFICATION OF SELF-CONCEPT AND CAREER MATURITY

Problem

The study aims to ascertain the relationship of self-concept, locus of control with career maturity of boys and girls.

Design

The present research is primarily a correlational research. However, for indepth study of career maturity in relation to sex, causal hypotheses were also framed. The purposes of a correlational study may be to determine relationship between variables or to use relationships in making predictions. In such type of studies, variables found not to be highly related are eliminated from further considerations, variables that are highly related may suggest causal comparative or experimental studies to determine, if the relationships are casual.

Variables

Following independent and dependent variables were taken in the present study.

Independent Variables

(a) Self-concept
(b) Locus of Control
(c) Sex

Dependent Variable

Career Maturity

(i) Attitudes Towards Career Maturity
(ii) Competencies of Career Maturity

Intervening Variables and Control

A systematic attempt was made to control intervening variance, through the identification of the intervening variables in the context and employing suitable methods of control.

I. Subject Related Variables	*Strategy of Control*
(a) Intelligence	Randomization
(b) Age	Elimination
(c) Education	Elimination
II. Situation Related Variables	
(a) Socio-Economic Status (SES)	Elimination
(b) Parents' Occupation Level	Elimination
(c) Caste	Delimitation

In addition to above mentioned intervening variables, there were following two variables, which could effect the results of the study:

1. Variations in test administrators
2. Variations in testing situations.

To control these two intervening variables, following things were exercised:

(a) The data was collected personally by the investigator.
(b) The data was collected in a classroom situation in a group which was selected randemly.
(c) Instructions and sequence of tests were kept similar for all the subjects.

Objectives

Main Objectives –

I. To examine the significant contribution of the variables of self-concept, locus of control and sex to predict career maturity.
II. To ascertain how self-concept, locus of control and sex are related to career maturity.
III. To investigate differences between boys and girls in relation to career maturity.

Secondary Objectives

I. To make an Indian adaptation of children's Nowickistrickland Locus of Control Scale.
II. To see whether Super's Self-concept Theory of Career Development is applicable in the Indian context.

Hypotheses

Following hypotheses were tested in the present study:

Major Hypotheses

Ho_I There will be no significant contribution of self-concept in predicting attitudes towards career maturity.

Ho_2 There will be no significant contribution of self-concept in predicting competencies of career maturity.

Ho_3 There will be no significant contribution of different dimensions of self-concept such as physical, social, temperamental, educational, moral and intellectual in predicting attitudes towards career maturity.

Ho_4 There will be no significant contribution of different dimensions of self-concept such as physical, social, temperamental, educational, moral and intellectual in predicting competencies of career maturity.

Ho_5 There will be no significant contribution of Locus of control in predicting attitudes towards career maturity.

Ho_6 There will be no significant contribution of locus of control in predicting competencies of career maturity.

Ho_7 There will be no significant contribution of sex in predicting attitudes towards career maturity.

Ho_8 There will be no significant contribution of sex in predicting competencies of career maturity.

Ho_9 There will be no significant relationship between self-concept and attitudes towards career maturity.

Ho_{10} There will be no significant relationship between dimensions of self-concept such as physical, social, temperamental, educational, moral and intellectual with attitudes towards career maturity.

Ho_{11} There will be no significant relationship between self-concept and competencies of career maturity.

Ho_{12} There will be no significant relationship between dimensions of self-concept such as physical, social, temperamental, educational, moral and intellectual with competencies of career maturity.

Ho_{13} There will be no significant relationship between locus of control (internality dimension) and attitudes towards career maturity.

Ho_{14} There will be no significant relationship between locus of control (internally dimension) and competencies of career maturity.

Ho_{15} There will be no difference between boys and girls in relation to their attitudes towards career maturity.

Ho_{16} There will be no difference between boys and girls in relation to their competencies of career maturity.

Sub-hypotheses

Following sub-hypotheses were also tested in the present study.

Self-concept as Predictor of Dimensions of Competence Scale of Career Maturity

Ho_1 No significant contribution of self-concept in predicting self-appraisal.

Ho$_{2}$ No significant contribution of self-concept in predicting occupational infermation.

Ho$_{3}$ No significant contribution of self-concept in predicting goal selection.

Ho$_{4}$ No significant contribution of self-concept in predicting planning.

Ho$_{5}$ No significant contribution of self-concept in predicting problem-solving.

Dimensions of Self-concept as a Predictor of Dimensions of Competence Scale of Career Maturity

Ho$_{6}$ No significant contribution of different dimensions of self-concept such as physical, social, temperamental, educational, moral and intellectual in predicting self-appraisal.

Ho$_{7}$ No significant contribution of different dimensions of self-concept such as physical, social, temperamental, educational, moral and intellectual in predicting occupational information.

Ho$_{8}$ No significant contribution of different dimensions of self-concept such as physical, social, temperamental, educational, moral and intellectual in predicting goal selection.

Ho$_{9}$ No significant contribution of different dimensions of self-concept such as physical, social, temperamental, educational, moral and intellectual in predicting planning.

Ho$_{10}$ No significant contribution of different dimensions of self-concept such as physical, social, temperamental, educational, moral and intellectual in predicting problem-solving.

Locus of Control as a Predictor of Dimensions of Competence Scale of Career Maturity

Ho$_{11}$ No significant contribution of locus of control in predicting self-appraisal.

Ho$_{12}$ No significant contribution of locus of control in predicting occupational information.

Ho$_{13}$ No significant contribution of locus of control in predicting goal selection.

Ho_{14} No significant contribution of locus of control in predicting planning.

Ho_{15} No significant contribution of locus of control in predicting problem solving.

Sex as a Predictor of Dimension of Competence Scale of Career Maturity

Ho_{16} No significant contribution of sex in predicting self-appraisal.

Ho_{17} No significant contribution of sex in predicting occupational information.

Ho_{18} No significant contribution of sex in predicting goal selection.

Ho_{19} No significant contribution of sex in predicting planning.

Ho_{20} No significant contribution of sex in predicting problem-solving.

Self-concept as Related to the Dimensions of Competence Scale of Career Maturity

Ho_{21} No significant relationship between self-concept and self-appraisal.

Ho_{22} No significant relationship between self-concept and occupational information.

Ho_{23} No significant relationship between self-concept and goal selection.

Ho_{24} No significant relationship between self-concept and planning.

Ho_{25} No significant relationship between self-concept and problem-solving.

Dimensions of Self-concept as Related to the Dimensions of Competence Scale of Career Maturity

Ho_{26} No significant relationship between dimensions of self-concept such as physical, social, temperamental, educational, moral and intellectual with self-appraisal.

Ho_{27} No significant relationship between dimensions of self concept such as physical, social, temperamental, educational, moral and intellectual with occupational information.

Ho_{28} No significant relationship between dimensions of self-concept such as physical, social, temperamental, educational, moral and intellectual with planning.

Ho_{29} No significant relationship between dimensions of self-concept such as physical, social, temperamental, educational, moral and intellectual with problem-solving.

Locus of Control as Related to the Dimensions of Competence Scale of Career Maturity

Ho_{31} No significant relationship between locus of control (internality dimension) and self-appraisal.

Ho_{32} No significant relationship between locus of control (internality dimension) and occupational information.

Ho_{33} No significant relationship between locus of control (internality dimension) and goal selection.

Ho_{34} No significant relationship between locus of control (internality dimension) and planning.

Ho_{35} No significant relationship between locus of control (internality dimension) and problem solving.

Difference Between Boys and Girls in Relation to the Dimensions of Competence Scale of Career Maturity

Ho_{36} No difference between boys and girls in relation to self-appraisal.

Ho_{37} No difference between boys and girls in relation to occupational information.

Ho_{38} No difference between boys and girls in relation to goal selection.

Ho_{39} No difference between boys and girls in relation to planning.

Ho_{40} No difference between boys and girls in relation to problem solving

4
PLAN AND PROCEDURE

Tools

To measure the variables included in the present research it was considered necessary to use scales/tests, which had been developed for the Indian children. The following published tests were available.

1. Self-Concept Questionnaire by Saraswat, R.K. (1984)

   Reliability : Test-retest reliability was .91.

   Validity : Content and construct validity was ascertained.

2. An Indian Adaptation of Career Maturity Inventory By Gupta. N. (1989)

   Reliability : Test-retest reliability was .78 to .82

   Validity : Content and construct validity was ascertained.

No suitable scale was available for measuring locus of control in the Indian sample of school children. Hence, the researcher took up the stupendous task of adapting Nowicki-strickland Locus of Control Scale (1973). Nowicki-Strickland accepting Rotter's definition of locus of control defines it as:

> "When a reinforcement is perceived by the subject as following some action of his own but not being entirely contingent upon his action, then, in our culture, it is typically perceived as the result of luck, chance, fate, as under the control of powerful others, or as

unpredictable because of the great complexity of the forces surrounding him. When the event is interpreted in this way by an individual, we have labelled this a belief in external control. If the person perceives that the event is contingent upon his own behaviour or his own relatively permanent characteristics, we have termed this a belief in internal control."

The scale is appropriate for children from ages 9 through 18. It consists of 40 items (See Appendix - B).

Indian Adaptation of Children's Nowicki-Strickland Internal-External Locus of Control Scale

Because, Children's Nowicki-Strickland Locus of Control Scale was in English and the norms were based on western culture. So, it was decided by the Investigator to make an Indian adaptation of it.

Steps

- The Nowicki-Strickland Locus of control scale was given to seven judges to check those items which were not applicable in Indian situation. These seven judges were teachers of DTE and DEPG & C OF NCERT. Five judges gave it back. According to three judges all items were applicable in Indian situation, while according to remaining two judges one item i.e. No. 21 (if you find a your leaf clover do you believe that it might bring you good luck?), need modification, as it was not considered to be culturally relevant. That item was modified in a desired way. जब कभी तुम आवश्यक कार्य से बाहर निकलते हो तो क्या रास्ते में किसी भरे बर्तन को देखना शुभ मानते हो?
- The back translation method was adopted for translating the test into Hindi. The test was given to five billingual experts (NCERT) to translate the test in Hindi. After a gap of two weeks, the same experts were given the Hindi translation made by them, and requested that they translate the test back

into English. After analyzing the translation (Hindi and English), it was found that there was no difference in the meaning of at the items of the test except the item No. 21.

➢ To assess the validity of Hindi versions, both versions of the test were administered to 100 students of Central Schools of Delhi. Those students were equally fluent in English and Hindi.

First, they were given the English version. Following instructions were given to the Central School subjects.

" We are trying to find out what boys and girls of your age think about certain things. Read each statement carefully. Put a tick (✓) under the 'yes' column, if you agree with the corresponding statement. Put a tick (✓) under the 'No' column if you disagree with the corresponding statement. There are no right and wrong answers. Don't take too much time in answering any one question but do try to answer them all."

Following day the same students were given the Hindi version of scale: निम्नलिखित निर्देश विद्यार्थियों को हिन्दी में दिये गये :

"हम यह ज्ञात करने का प्रयत्न कर रहे हैं कि आपकी उम्र के लड़के/लड़कियाँ कुछ चीजों के बारे में क्या सोचते हैं। प्रत्येक वाक्य को ध्यानपूर्वक पढ़िये, यदि आप उस वाक्य से सहमत हैं तो "हाँ" के नीचे बने खाने में सही (✓) का चिन्ह लगाये और यदि आप उस वाक्य से असहमत हैं तो "नही" के नीचे बने खाने में गलत (X) का चिन्ह लगायें। कोई भी जवाब सही या गलत नहीं है। किसी भी वाक्य का उत्तर देने की कोशिश कीजिए।"

		हाँ	नहीं
1.	क्या तुम्हें विश्वास है कि अधिकांश समस्याएं हल हो जाएगी अगर तुम उनके साथ खिलवाड़ न करो?	( )	( )
2.	क्या तुम्हें विश्वास है कि तुम अपने आपको जुकाम होने से बचा सकते हो?	( )	( )
3.	क्या कुछ बच्चे जन्म से ही भाग्यशाली होते हैं?	( )	( )

		हाँ	नहीं
4.	क्या अक्सर तुम यह अनुभव करते हो कि अच्छे अंक प्राप्त करना तुम्हारे लिए बहुत महत्व रखता है?	( )	( )
5.	क्या तुम अक्सर उन बातों के लिए दोषी ठहराये जाते हो जिसमें कि तुम्हारा दोष नहीं होता है?	( )	( )
6.	क्या तुमको यह विश्वास है कि अगर कोई कड़ी मेहनत करे तो वह किसी भी विषय में सफलता प्राप्त कर सकता है?	( )	( )
7.	क्या तुम यह अनुभव करते हो कि अधिकांशतः कड़ी मेंहनत करने से कुछ नहीं होता क्योंकि उसका उचित फल नहीं मिलता है?	( )	( )
8.	क्या तुम ऐसा सोचते हो अगर प्रातःकाल की शुरूआत अच्छी होगी तो सारा दिन अच्छा बीतेगा, चाहे तुम कुछ भी करो।	( )	( )
9.	क्या तुम यह समझते हो कि प्रायः माता-पिता अपने बच्चों की बातों को सुनते हैं?	( )	( )
10.	क्या तुम्हें विश्वास है कि इच्छा करने से चीजों को अच्छा बनाया जा सकता है?	( )	( )
11.	जब कभी तुम्हें दण्ड दिया जाता है तो तुम्हें ऐसा लगता है कि यह बिना किसी कारण के दिया गया है?	( )	( )
12.	क्या अधिकाशतः तुम अपने मित्रों के विचारों में परिर्वतन लाने में कठिनाई का अनुभव करते हो?	( )	( )
13.	क्या तुम सोचते हो कि टीम के विजयी होने के लिए हौसला किस्मत से ज्यादा साहयक होता है?	( )	( )
14.	क्या तुम्हें अपने माता-पिता के किसी भी तरह के विचारों में परिवर्तन लाना असंभव होता है।	( )	( )
15.	क्या तुम सोचते हो कि तुम्हारे माता-पिता को तुम्हें अधिकतर निर्णय स्वयं लेने की स्वतन्त्रता देनी चाहिए?	( )	( )

		हाँ	नहीं
16.	क्या तुम सोचते हो कि जब तुम गलत कार्य करते हो तब तुम उसको कम ही सही कर पाते हो?	( )	( )
17.	क्या तुम्हें विश्वास है कि कुछ बच्चे जन्म से ही खेलों में अच्छे होते हैं?	( )	( )
18.	क्या तुम्हारी उम्र के दूसरे बच्चे तुमसे ज्यादा ताकतवर हैं?	( )	( )
19.	क्या तुम सोचते हो कि अधिकांश समस्याओं का सबसे अच्छा समाधान यह है कि उसके विषय में कुछ सोचा ही नहीं जाय?	( )	( )
20.	क्या तुम सोचते हो कि तुम्हें अपने मित्रों का चयन करने के लिए चुनाव की काफी स्वतंत्रता हैं?	( )	( )
21.	जब कभी तुम आवश्यक कार्य से बाहर निकलते हो तो रास्ते में किसी भरे बर्तन को देखना शुभ मानते हैं?	( )	( )
22.	क्या तुम ऐसा सोचते हो कि तुम्हें जो अंक मिले हैं वह तुम्हारे से बहुत अधिक सम्बन्धित है?	( )	( )
23.	क्या तुम सोचते हो कि जब तुम्हारी उम्र का कोई बच्चा तुम्हें मारने का निर्णय लेता है तो तुम उसको कम हीं रोक पाते हो?	( )	( )
24.	क्या तुम्हारे पास कोई ऐसी वस्तु है जिसके कारण तुम्हें हमेशा सफलता मिलती है?	( )	( )
25.	क्या तुम सोचते हो कि लोग तुम्हें पसन्द करते हैं या नापसंद यह तुम्हारे द्वारा किये गये कार्यों पर निर्भर करता है?	( )	( )
26.	अगर तुम्हारे माता-पिता तुम्हारी सहायता करेंगे अगर तुम उन्हें ऐसा करने के लिए कहोगे?	( )	( )
27.	क्या तुमने यह अनुभव किया है कि लोगों ने तुम्हारे प्रति बिना किसी कारण के अभद्र व्यवहार किया है?	( )	( )

		हाँ	नहीं
28.	क्या तुम ऐसा सोचते हो कि आज जो कुछ तुम कर रहे हो उससे कल जो होने वाला है उन्हें तुम परिर्वतन कर सकते हो?	( )	( )
29.	क्या तुम इस बात में विश्वास करते हो कि जब कोई बुरी घटना होने को रही हो तो वो होकर ही रहेगी चाहे तुम उसको रोकने की कितनी भी कोशिश करते रहें?	( )	( )
30.	क्या तुम ऐसा सोचते हो कि बच्चे जो कुछ भी करना चाहें वह कर सकते हैं अगर वह निरंतर कोशिश करते रहें?	( )	( )
31.	क्या तुम्हें ऐसा लगता है कि घर पर जो कुछ तुम करना चाहते हो उसकी काशिश करना व्यर्थ है?	( )	( )
32.	क्या तुम सोचते हो कि कोई भी अच्छी घटना कठिन परिश्रम के फलस्वरूप होती है?	( )	( )
33.	क्या तुम ऐसा सोचते हो कि जब कोई हम उम्र तुम्हारा दुश्मन होना चाहता हो तो तुम उस स्थिति को बदलने में कम ही कुछ कर पाते हो?	( )	( )
34.	क्या तुम ऐसा सोचते हो कि मित्रों से जो कुछ तुम करवाना चाहते हो वो करवाना आसान है?	( )	( )
35.	क्या तुम अक्सर यह अनुभव करते हो कि घर पर तुम्हें जो कुछ खाने के लिए मिलता है उसके लिए तुम कुछ कम ही कर सकते हो?	( )	( )
36.	क्या तुम अक्सर यह अनुभव करते हो कि जब तुम्हें कोई पसंद नही करता है तो तुम इस बारे में कुछ कम ही कर सकते हो?	( )	( )
37.	क्या तुम अक्सर यह अनुभव करते हो कि स्कूल में कोशिश करना व्यर्थ है क्योंकि अधिकतर बच्चे तुमसे ज्यादा होशियार हैं?	( )	( )

		हाँ	नहीं
38.	क्या तुम इस तरह के व्यक्ति जो इस बात में विश्वास रखते हैं कि पूर्व योजना के परिणाम अच्छे होते हैं?	( )	( )
39.	क्या तुम अक्सर यह अनुभव करते हो कि तुम्हारे परिवार में जो निर्णय लिए जाते हैं उसमें तुम कुछ कम ही कह पाते हो?	( )	( )
40.	क्या तुम सोचते हो कि होशियार होना भाग्यवान होने से ज्यादा अच्छा है?	( )	( )

English verison of the test was given in the appendix–B.

Scoring of the Test: The total score is the total number of items answered in an externally controlled direction (Externally keyed response sheet was given in the Appendix – D). The range of the score is 0-40. Total score of a test is treated as a raw score of a test. 'r' was computed between the raw scores of both the tests, which was found. 56.

Estimating Validity and Reliability of the Scale Validity

Content Validity – Most of the items of the adapted locus of control scale were of original locus of control scale items with only slight modifications. The modified items have also been discussed at length with experts in the area of psychology regarding their suitability for Indian students.

Construct Validity – The test has construct validity also. Because, this test is correlated with its English version (original test), which has construct validity. So, it was assumed that this also has construct validity.

Reliability

A test-retest reliability with an interval of one month was calculated on Indian sample (N=97) drawn from class XI, was found .56.

Norms:

The Indian norms for the locus of control scale were based on scores obtained on a sample of 736 students (Boys and Girls) of class XI of Government Senior Secondary School of Delhi.

The mean and standard deviation (SD) for boys and girls separately was computed for developing the norms, which is shown in the following table.

Table 4.1
Mean and SD of Boys and Girls (N = 736)

Sex	*Mean*	*SD*	*Mid value* (± O)	*Internal*	*External*
Boys	13.05	3.99	9.06 to 16.04	9.06 or Below 9.06	16.04 or above 16.04
Girls	12.07	5.87	6.20 to 17.94	6.20 or Below 6.20	17.94 or above 17.94

The norms of this test were based on mean and ± SD.

For boys we got the mean value of 13.05 and SD 3.99. By adding ± SD (3.99) to mean value (13.05) we found the mid values i.e. 9.06 to 16.04. So, those boys who scored 9.00 or below 9.00 were termed as internal and those who scored 16.00 or above 16.00 were termed as externals. Similarly in the case of girls by adding ± SD (5.87) to mean value (12.07) we found the mid values i.e. 6.20 to 17.94. So those girls who scored 6.00 or above 6.00 were termed as internals and those who scored 18.00 or above 18.00 were termed as externals.

In both cases those who lie in middle value or average i.e. for boys from 9.06 to 16.04 (9.00 to 16.00) and for girls from 6.20 to 17.94 (6.00 to 18.00) were not taken because in the present study, investigator dealt with two extremes i.e. internal and external.

Nowicki-Strickland also computed mean and SD for boys and girls separately, for developing the norms, which is shown in the following table.

Table 4.2
Mean and SD of Boys and Girls (N = 152)

Sex	*Mean*	*SD*
Boys	12.48	4.81
Girls	12.01	5.51

Mean and SD presented in Tables 4.1 and 4.2 indicate that Indian boys are more external (M = 13.05) in comparison to the Western boys (M=12.48), While there is no difference between Indian girls and Western girls in relation to it.

Sample

The sample of the study was selected through *Cluster Random Sampling*. In the present study the defined population consisted of XI class boys and girls of Government Schools of Delhi. It was not feasible to take all the XI class students of government schools of Delhi. So, for the selection of the sample, first of all relevant information about the number of government schools of Delhi was collected from State Council of Educational Research and Training. A list of schools was obtained from SCERT. All the schools were divided into four zones in that list. Two zones, i.e. (I) South Delhi and (ii) West Delhi, were selected randomly from the list, Again by random selection of all the schools in these two zones twelve schools were chosen. Data was collected on a total 700 boys and girls, which were reduced finally to 582, as the incomplete and casually responded sheets were not taken into account. Course-wise and sex-wise distribution of the final sample is presented below.

Table 4.3
Sex-wise Distribution of the Students in the Academic Stream

S.No.	*Academic Stream*	*Boys*	*Girls*	
1.	Arts	187	169	
2.	Commerce	75	60	
3.	Science	54	37	
	Total	316	266	582

Procedure:

Data was collected by taking following steps:

- Investigator had gone to schools and sought permission from the authorities, which was granted. All the principals, except one, provided all the help that the investigator asked for.
- After taking permission from principals investigator contacted the teachers and fixed a time for administering tests.
- Self-concept Questionnaire, Indian adaptation of Career Maturity Inventory and Indian adaptation of Locus of Control Scale were administered on 700 subjects of twelve government senior secondary schools of Delhi.
- The squence of administering tests and time taken for completing each test was as follows:

	Name of Test	*Duration*
i)	Career Maturity Inventory	80-90 mts.
ii)	Self-concept Questionnaire	15-20 mts.
iii)	Locus of Control Scale	10-15 mts.

- All the instruments were completed in a group situation by the students in the classroom.
- The total data was collected in two months between January to March 1991.

Statistical Methodology

Following statistical techniques were employed:

- The multiple regression analysis was used to see

the maximum contribution of independent variables to dependent variables.

- Person's Product Moment Correlation was computed between all the variables.
- T-test was computed to see the significant difference between boys and girls in relation to the career maturity.

5

ANALYSIS AND INTERPRETATION OF THE RESULTS

The major aims of the study were: (i) to investigate the contribution of self-concept, locus of control and sex in predicting career maturity; (ii) to see how self-concept, locus of control and sex are related to career maturity: (iii) to examine the significant difference between boys and girls in relation to career maturity.

Sixteen major and forty sub-null hypotheses presented in Chapter IV were tested for their statistical significance. A multiple regression analysis, product-moment correlation and t-test techniques were employed to analyze and interpret the data. Analysis of the data was done by the computer. The .01 and .05 level of significance were sued throughout the analysis.

A list of all the variables and their abbreviation is presented in the Table 5.4.

Table 5.1
List of Variables

S.No.	*Variable*	*Abbreviation*
1.	Sex	Sex
2.	Self-concept	SC
3.	Physical Self-concept	Phy.SC
4.	Social Self-concept	Soc.SC
5.	Temperamental self-concept	Tem.SC
6.	Educational Self-concept	Edu.SC
7.	Moral Self-concept	Mor.SC
8.	Intellectual Self-concept	Int.SC
9.	Locus of Control	LOC
10.	Attitude towards career maturity	Att.Towards CM
11.	Self-Appraisal	SA
12.	Occupational Information	OI
13.	Goal Selection	GS
14.	Planning	Plann.
15.	Problem Solving	PS

Table 5.2
Mean and Standard Deviation of Self-concept, Different Dimension of Self-concept, Locus of Control, Attitudes Towards Career Maturity, Competence Scale of Career Maturity and Dimension of competence Scale of Career Maturity

(N=582)

S.No.	*Variable*	*Mean*	*SD*
1.	Self-concept (Total)	177.113	17.588
2.	Physical self-concept	28.826	3.996
3.	Social self-concept	29.218	3.551
4.	Moral self-concept	30.534	3.963
5.	Intellectual self-concept	30.976	5.328
6.	Educational self-concept	31.005	3.412
7.	Temperamental self-concept	26.819	4.255
8.	Locus of control	10.344	5.778
9.	Attitudes towards career maturity	30.749	6.667
10.	Competence test (Total)	39.593	8.681
11.	Self-appraisal	8.448	2.225
12.	Occupational information	8.859	2.403
13.	Goal selection	8.450	2.270
14.	Planning	7.285	2.732
15.	Problem solving	6.555	2.198

Note: Results of different variables showed in following tables are arranged inorder of high to low significant values.

Table 5.3

Multiple Regression Analysis Predicting Attitudes Towards Career Maturity from Dimension of Self-concept, Locus of Control and Sex

N = 582.

Sl. No.	*Independent Variables (IV)*	*Dependent Variable (DV)*		*Attitudes towards Career Maturity*	
		R^2	*RSQ*	*Beta*	*F-value*
1.	LOC	0.054	0.054	-0.195	17.07**
2.	Phy.SC	0.061	0.007	0.069	1.86 n.s.
3.	Tem. SC	0.064	0.003	0.063	1.62 n.s.
4.	Soc.SC	0.065	0.001	0.051	1.15 n.s.
5.	Mor. SC	0.066	0.001	-0.045	0.69 n.s.
6.	Sex	0.067	0.0003	-0.017	0.16 n.s.
7.	Edu.SC	0.067	0.0001	-0.012	0.06 n.s.

Multiple R = 0.258
R Square = 0.668
** *Significant at .01 level*

Table 5.3 reveals that the final multiple correlation with the criterion (attitudes towards career maturity) was R = 0.258. This multiple correlation accounted for 6.7% of the variance in the prediction of attitudes towards career maturity. The first variable, i.e. LOC accounted for 5.4% of the variance with attitudes towards career maturity. The variable intellectual self-concept did not enter into the equation because the tolerance level was insufficient for further computation and as a result the regression was stopped.

Table 5.3 reveals that major null hypothesis No. V was rejected, as the obtained F-value (17.07>.01) was significant at. 01 level. This indicates that LOC (internality dimension) has a significant contribution in the prediction of attitudes towards career maturity.

Table 5.3 also shows that the major null Hypothesis

No. III and VII are retained, as the yielded F-values for Phy. SC (1.86<.05); Tem. SC (1.62<.05); Soc. SC (1.15<.05); Mor. SC (0.69<.05); Sex (0.16 <.05); Edu. SC (0.06<.05) are not statistically significant. It indicates that these variables have no significant contribution in the prediction of attitudes towards career maturity.

Table 5.4

Multiple Regression Analysis Predicting Self-appraisal from Dimensions of Self-concept, Locus of Control and Sex

Sl. No.	*Independent Variables*	*Dependent: Self-Appraisal (Dimension of Variable Competence Scale)*			
		R^2	*RSQ*	*Beta*	*F-value*
1.	LOC	0.097	0.097	-0.215	22.74**
2.	Edu.SC	0.134	0.011	0.158	11.65**
3.	Soc. SC	0.123	0.026	0.151	11.25**
4.	Sex	0.146	0.012	0.106	6.76**
5.	Int.SC	0.153	0.008	-0.101	4.64**
6.	Phy.SC	0.154	0.001	0.051	1.06 n.s.
7.	Tem. SC	0.155	0.0006	-0.029	0.38 n.s.
8.	Mor. SC	0.155	0.00006	-0.010	0.03 n.s.

Multiple R = 0.393 *Significant at .01 level*
R Square = 0.155 **Significant at .05 level*

Table 5.4 reveals that the final multiple correlation with the criterion (Self-Appraisal) is R = 0.393. This multiple correlation accounted for 15.5% of the variance in the prediction of SA. Locus of control alone accounted for 9.7% of the variance with the SA. Soc. SC and Edu. SC accounted for 2.6%, 1.1% of the variance respectively with SA. Sex accounted for 1.2% of the variance with SA. Next four independent variables such as Int. SC., Phy. SC, Tem. SC and Mor. SC accounted for .88% (Summated) of the variance.

Table 5.4 also shows that the sub-null Hypothesis

No. 11 and 16 are rejected, because the yielded F-values for LOC (22.74> .01) and for Sex (6.76>.01) are significant at .01 level. It means that LOC and Sex have a significant contribution in the prediction of SA.

Sub null Hypothesis No. 6 is partially rejected, because the three dimension of self-concept such as Int. (4.64>. 05): Soc. (11.25>.01) and Edu. (11.64>.01) have significant contribution in predicting SA. While remaining three dimensions of self-concept such as Phy. (1.06<.05); Tem. (0.38 <.05) and Mor. (0.03 <.05) have no contribution in predicting SA.

Table 5.5

Multiple Regression Analysis Predicting Occupational Information from Dimensions of Self-concept Locus of Control and Sex.

Sl. No.	*Independent Variables*	*Dependent Variable: Occupational Information (Dimension of Competence Scale)*			
		R^2	*RSQ*	*Beta*	*F-value*
1.	LOC	0.095	0.095	-0.198	19.06**
2.	Edu.SC	0.129	0.035	0.159	11.6**
3.	Soc.SC	0.141	0.011	0.094	4.36*
4.	Mor.SC	0.143	0.002	0.079	2.23 n.s.
5.	Int. SC	0.146	0.003	-0.066	1.99 n.s.
6.	Phy.SC	0.147	0.001	0.056	1.27 n.s.
7.	Sex	0.149	0.001	0.037	0.81 n.s.
8.	Tem.SC	0.149	0.0003	-0.023	0.23 n.s.

Multiple R = 0.386 — ***Significant at .01 level*

R Square = 0.149 — **Significant at .05 level*

Table 5.5 reveals that the final multiple correlation with the criterion (occupational information) is R= 0.386). This multiple correlation accounted for 14.9% of the variance in the prediction of OI. Locus of control accounted for 9.5% of the variance in the prediction of OI. Educational Self-concept and Soc. SC accounted for 3.5% and 1.1% respectively. The remaining five variables such as Mor. SC, Int. SC, Phy. SC, Sex and Tem. SC added another 0.82%.

Table 5.5 also depicts that sub null Hypothesis no. 12 is rejected, as the obtained F-value for LOC (19.06> .01) is significant at .01 level. This indicates that LOC (internality dimension) has a significant contribution in the prediction of OI.

The sub null Hypothesis No. 17 is retained, beause the obtained F-value (0.81<.05) for sex is not significant. It means that this variable does not significantly contribute in the prediction of OI.

Table 5.5 reveals that the sub null Hypothesis No. 7 is partially accepted, because the two dimensions of self-concept i.e. Edu. SC (11.6>.01) and Soc. SC (4.36>.05) have significant contribution in the prediction of OI, while the remaining four variables such as Mor. SC (2.23<.05): Int. SC (1.99<.05): Phy. SC (1.27<.05); Tem. SC (.23<.05) have no significant contribution in the prediction of OI.

Table 5.6

Multiple Regression Analysis Predicting Goal Selection from Dimension of Self-concept, Locus of Control and Sex

Sl. No.	*Independent Variables*	*Dependent Variables : Goal Selection (Dimension of Competence Scale)*			
		R^2	*RSC*	*Beta*	*F-value*
1.	LOC	0.147	0.147	-0.245	31.11**
2.	Mor.SC	0.175	0.029	0.101	5.38*
3.	Soc.SC	0.188	0.012	0.092	5.34*
4.	Sex	0.194	0.006	0.101	3.88*
5.	Edu. SC	0.199	0.006	0.075	2.76 n.s.
6.	Phy.SC	0.202	0.003	0.065	1.85 n.s.
7.	Int. SC	0.202	0.003	0.025	0.31 n.s.
8.	Tem.SC	0.203	0.003	-0.023	0.25 n.s.

Multiple R = 0.451 ***Significant at .01 level;*
R Square = 0.203 **Significant at .05 level.*

Table 5.6 reveals that the final multiple correlation with the criterion (Goal selection) is R =.451. This multiple correlation acounted for 20.3% of the variance in the prediction of goal selection. Table shows that the LOC alone accounted for 14.7% of the variance with the goal selection. Next three variables such as Mor. SC, Soc, SC and sex accounted for an additional 4.71% of the variance. While the remaining four variables such as Edu. SC, Phy. SC, Int. SC., and Tem. SC added only 0.89%.

Resulted in Table 5.6 reveals that the sub null Hypothesis No. 18 and 13 are rejected, because the obtained F-values for Sex (5.34>.05) and LOC (31.11>.01) are significant. This indicates that Sex and LOC have significant contribution in the prediction of goal selection.

Table 5.6 also shows that the sub null Hypothesis No. 8 is partially rejected, because Soc. SC (5.38)>.05) and Mor. SC (3.88>.05) are the significant contributor of GS, while other four dimensions of self concept such as Edu. SC (2.76<.05), Phy. SC (1.85<.05), Int, SC (.31<.05), Tem. SC (.25<.05) have no significant contribution in the prediction of GS.

Table 5.7: Multiple Regression Analysis Predicting Planning from Dimensions of Self-concept, Locus of Control and Sex

Sl. No.	*Independent Variables*	*Dependent: Planning (Dimension of Variable Competence Scale)*			
		R^2	*RSC*	*Beta*	*F-value*
1.	LOC	0.113	0.113	-0.171	15.02**
2.	Sex	0.179	0.019	0.151	14.35**
3.	Phy.SC	0.159	0.046	0.176	13.58**
4.	Soc.SC	0.190	0.004	0.063	2.09 n.s.
5.	Edu. SC	0.193	0.0006	0.061	1.44 n.s.
6.	Tem. SC	0.186	0.004	0.047	1.04n.s.
7.	Int. SC	0.192	0.002	0.029	0.44 n.s.

Multiple R = 0.439 *Significant at .01 level
R Square = 0.193

Table 5.7 reveals that the final multiple correlation with the criterian (planning) is R = 0.439. This multiple correlation accounted for 19.3% of the variance in the prediction of planning. Locus of control alone accounted for 11.3% of the variance with planning. Phy. SC accounted for 4.6% and Sex accounted for 1.9% of the variance with planning. Another four dimensions of Self-concept.

i.e. Mor., Soc., Tem. and Int. added another 1.42% of the variance.

Educational self-concept did not enter into the equation because the tolerance level was insufficient for the further computation and as a result the regression was stopped.

Results presented in Table 5.7 reveals that sub null Hypothesis No. 19 and 14 are rejected, because the yielded F-values for Sex (14.35>.01) and LOC (15.02>.01) are significant at .01 level. It means that Sex and LOC have a significant contribution in the prediction of planning.

Table 5.7 also shows that the sub null Hypothesis No. 9 is partially rejected because Phy. SC (13.58>.01) has a significant contribution in the prediction of planning, while other four dimensions of self-concept such as Moral Self-concept (1.44<.05), Soc. SC (2.09<.05), Tem. SC (1.04<.05), Int. SC (0.44<.05) have no significant contribution in the prediction of planning.

Table 5.8

Multiple Regression Analysis Predicting Problem Solving from Dimensions of Self-concept, Locus of Control and Sex

Sl. No.	*Independent Variables*	*Dependent: Problem Solving (Dimension Variable of Competence Scale)*			
		R^2	*RSQ*	*Beta*	*F-value*
1.	Sex	0.207	0.037	0.243	41.14**
2.	LOC	0.170	0.170	-0.222	28.03**
3.	Mor. SC	0.272	0.0003	0.134	7.43**
4.	Phy. SC	0.266	0.011	0.089	3.88*
5.	Int. SC	0.272	0.0009	0.057	1.72 n.s.
6.	Soc. SC	0.271	0.002	0.049	1.39 n.s.
7.	Tem. SC	0.255	0.048	0.036	0.67 n.s.
8.	Edu.SC	0.269	0.004	0.022	0.26 n.s.

Multiple R = 0.522 — ***Significant at .01 level*

R Square = 0.273 — **Significant at .05 level*

Table 5.8 reveals that the multiple correlation with

the criterion (problem solving) is R = 0.522. This multiple correlation acounted for 27.3% of the variance in the prediction of problem solving. Locus of control accounted for 17% of the variance. Sex accounted for 3.7% of the variance. Mor. SC and Phy. SC accounted for 4.8% and 1.1% of the variance respectively. The remaining four dimensions, i.e. Int. SC., Soc,. SC. Tem. SC. and Edu. SC. added another. 72% of the variance in the prediction of criterion.

Results presented in Table 5.8 reveals that the sub null Hypothesis No. 20 and 15 are rejected, Because the obtained F-value for Sex (41.14>.01) and LOC (28.03>.01) are significant at .01 level. It means that Sex and LOC have a significant contribution in the prediction of problem solving.

Table 5.8 indicates that the sub null Hypothesis No. 10 is partially rejected, because out of six, two dimensions of self-concept such as Mor. (7.43>.01) and Phy. (3.88>.05) are the significant contributors of problem solving. While remaining four dimensions of self concept such as Int. (1.72 .05) Soc. (1.39 <.05), Tem. (0.67<.05) and Edu. (0.26<.05) have no significant contribution in the prediction of problem solving.

Table 5.9
Multiple Regression Analysis Predicting Competencies of Career Maturity (total) from Dimensions of Self-concept, Locus of Control and Sex

Sl. No.	*Independent Variables*	*Dependent: Variable*	*Competencies of Career Maturity (Total)*		
		R^2	*RSQ*	*Beta*	*F-value*
1.	LOC	0.228	0.228	-0.287	51.56**
2.	Sex	0.315	0.019	0.166	21.1**
3.	Phy.SC	0.276	0.427	0.132	11.18**
4.	Soc.SC	0.296	0.020	0.127	9.12**
5.	Edu. SC	0.328	0.013	0.112	7.39**
6.	Mor.SC	0.333	0.004	0.092	3.92*
7.	Int. SC	0.333	0.0002	-0.017	0.17 n.s.

Multiple R = 0.577 **Significant at .01 level
R Square = 0.333 **Significant at .05 level*

Table 5.9 reveals that the multiple correlation with the criterion (competencies of career maturity total) is R= 0.577. This multiple correlation accounted for 33.3% of the variance in the prediction of competences of career maturity. Locus of control accounted for 22.8% of the variance, while Soc. SC and Phy. SC accounted for 4.7% and 2.01% respectively. Sex accounted for 1.9% of the variance. Another three dimensions of self-concept i.e. Edu., Mor., and Int. added another 1.81% of the variance in the prediction of criterion.

Temperamental self-concept did not enter into the equation because the tolerance level was insufficient for the further computation and as a result the regression was stopped.

Results presented in Table 5.9 reveals that the major null Hypothesis No. VIII and VI are rejected, because the obtained F-value for Sex (21.1>.01) and LOC (51.56 >.01) are significant at .01 level. It means that the sex and LOC have significant contribution in the prediction of competencies of career maturity.

Table 5.9 also reveals that the major null Hypothesis No. IV is partially retained, because the obtained F-value for Int. SC (0.17<.05) is not significant. On the other hand, remaining four dimensions of self-concept such as Soc. (11.18>.01), Phy. (9.12>.01). Edu. (7.39>.01), Int.(3.92>.05) have significant contribution in the prediction of competencies of career maturity.

Table 5.10 reveals that the major null Hypothesis No. I is retained, because self-concept has no significant contribution (6.021%) in the prediction of attitudes towards career maturity. Major null Hypothesis No. II and sub Hypothesis No. 1, 2, 3, 4 & 5 are rejected because self-concept has a significant contribution in the prediction of SA (11.32%), OI (12.93), GS (19.19%), Planning (12.6%), PS (22.09%) and total competencies of career maturity (30.07%). All the values are significant at .01 level.

Table 5.10

Predicting Attitudes Towards Career Maturity, Dimensions of Competence Scale of Career Maturity and Total Competencies of Career Maturity from Self-Concept

N = 582.

Independent Variable	*Dependent Variable :* Attitude Scale of Career Maturity		*Attitude Scale of Career Maturity, Competence Scale of Career Maturity and Its Dimensions* — Competence Scale and Its Dimensions: *SA*		*OI*		*GS*		*Plan*		*PS*		*Total*	
	r	R^2	*r*	R^2	*r*	R^2	*r*	R^2	*r*	R^2	*r*	R^2	*r*	R^2
Self-Concept (total)	0.1753	0.0602	0.2563	0.1132	0.3063	0.1293	0.3649	0.1919	0.3550	0.1260	0.3894	0.2209	0.4583	0.3007

SA = Self-Appraisal
OI = Occupational Information
GS = Goal Selection
Plan = Planning
PS = Problem Solving
** *Significant at .01 level*

Table 5.11
Sex–wise Mean and Standard Deviation of Self-concept, Different Dimensions of Self-concept, Locus of Control, Attitudes Towards Career Maturity, Competence Scale of Career Maturity and Dimension of Competence Scale of Career Maturity.

Sl. Variables	Boys		Girls	
	Mean	SD	Mean	SD
1. Self-concept (total)	177.22	18.68	176.99	16.23
2. Phy. SC	28.96	4.36	28.67	3.51
3. Soc. SC	28.92	3.72	28.57	3.32
4. Mor. SC	30.90	4.15	30.09	3.69
5. Int. SC	31.19	6.18	30.72	4.09
6. Edu. SC	31.09	3.64	30.90	3.12
7.Tem. SC	26.55	4.29	27.13	4.19
8. LOC	11.57	4.86	8.89	6.42
9.Att. Towards CM	30.51	6.96	31.03	6.31
10.Com. Test (total)	37.78	9.08	41.75	7.65
11.SA	8.11	2.38	8.85	1.95
12.OI	8.68	2.61	9.06	2.12
13. G	8.16	2.62	8.79	1.72
14.Plann	6.82	2.76	7.84	2.59
15. PS	5.98	2.15	7.23	2.06

Among Boys

Table 5.12
Multiple Regression Analysis Predicting Attitudes Towards Career Maturity from Dimensions of Self-concept, Locus of Control for Boys

(N = 316)

Sl. No.	Independent Variables	Dependent Variable Attitude Towards Career Maturity			
		R^2	RSQ	Beta	F-value
1.	LOC	0.027	0.027	-0.176	8.42**
2.	Mor. SC	0.032	0.005	0.140	3.62 n.s.
3.	Phy.SC	0.040	0.008	0.076	1.11n.s.
4.	Tem. SC	0.043	0.003	0.062	0.81n.s.
5.	Soc. SC	0.045	0.002	0.053	0.66 n.s.
6.	Int. SC	0.046	0.001	-0.035	0.27n.s.
7.	Edu. SC	0.046	0.0001	-0.012	0.03 n.s.

Multiple R = 0.215
R^2 = 0.046

***Significant at .01*

The final multiple correlation with the criterion (Attitudes Towards CM) is R = 0.215. This multiple correlation accounted for 4.6% of the variance in the prediction of atti. Towards CM. Locus of control accounted for 2.7% of the variance with attitudes towards CM. Phy. SC, Mor. SC, and Tem. SC accounted for .77%, .54%, and 29% of the variance respectively, Remaining three variables, i.e. Soc., SC, Int, SC and Edu. SC added .31% of the variance.

Table 5.12 reveals that the major null Hypothesis No. V is rejected in the case of boys, as the obtained F-value (8.42>.01) is significant at .01 level. This indicates that LOC (internality dimension) has a significant contribution in the prediction of attitudes towards career maturity for boys.

Table 5.12 also depicts that the major null Hypothesis No. III is retained, as the yielded F-values for Mor. SC (3.62<.05); Phy. SC (1.11<.05). Tem. SC (0.81<.05); Soc. SC (0.66<.05); Int. SC (0.27<.05) and Edu. SC (0.03<.05) are not satistically significant. It means that these variables have no significant contribution in the prediction of attitudes towards career maturity, for boys.

Table 5.13
Multiple Regression Analysis Predicting Self-Appraisal from Dimension of Self-concept and Locus of Control for Boys

(N = 316)

Sl. No.	*Independent Variables*	*Dependent Variable: Self-Appraisal (Dimension of Competence Scale)*			
		R^2	*RSQ*	*Beta*	*F-value*
1.	LOC	0.112	0.112	-0.298	28.62**
2.	Soc. SC	0.136	0.023	0.168	7.73**
3.	Edu. SC	0.144	0.008	0.179	7.67**
4.	Int. SC	0.162	0.018	-0.144	5.24*
5.	Tem. SC	0.164	0.002	-0.041	0.45 n.s.
6.	Mor. SC	0.165	0.0005	-0.029	0.20 n.s.

Multiple R = 0.406   ***Significant at .01 level*

R Square = 0.165   ** Significant at .05 level*

Table 5.13 reveals that the final multiple correlation with the criterion (self-appraisal) is R=0.406. This multiple correlation accounted for 16.5% of the variance in the prediction of SA. Locus of control accounted for 11.2% of the variance. Social Self-concept and Int. SC accounted for 2.63% and 1.83% of the variance respectively. Remaining three variables. i.e. Mor. SC, Edu. SC and Tem. SC added 1.11% (summated) of the variance. The variable physical self-concept did not enter into the equation. Because the tolerance leavel was insufficient for further computation, and as a result the regression was stopped.

Table 5.13 shows that the sub null Hypothesis No. 11 is rejected, in the case of boys, as the obtained F-value for LOC ((28.62>.01) is significant at .01 level. It means that LOC has a significant contribution in the prediction of SA, for boys.

Table 5.13 also depicts that the sub nulls Hypothesis No. 6 in the case of boys, is partially retained because the two dimensions of self-concept i.e. Tem. SC (0.45<.05); and Mor. SC (0.20<.05) have no significant contribution in the prediction of SA. While the other two variables i.e. Soc. SC (7.73>.01); Edu. SC (7.67>.01) are significant at .01 level and another dimension of self-concept i.e. Int. SC (5.24<.05) is significant at .05 level. Therefore, these three variables have a significant contribution in the prediction of SA, for boys.

The final multiple correlation with the criterion (occupational information) is R=0.382. This multiple correlation accounted for 14.6% of the variance in the prediction of OI. Locus of control accounted for 10.8% of the variance. Educational self-concept accounted for 2.3% of the variance. Another four dimensions of self-concept, i.e. Soc. SC, Mor. SC, Int. SC and Phy. SC added total 1.44% of the variance. The variable Tem. SC did not enter into the equation because the tolerance level was insufficient for further computation, and, as a result the regression was stopped.

Table 5.14

Multiple Regression Analysis Predicting Occupational Information from Dimensions of Self-concept and Locus of Control for Boys

(N =316).

Sl. No.	*Independent Variables*	*Dependent Variable: Occupational Informations (Dimension of Competence Scale)*			
		R^2	*RSQ*	*Beta*	*F-value*
1.	LOC	0.108	0.108	-0.259	20.72**
2.	Edu. SC	0.131	0.023	0.107	2.78 n.s
3.	Soc. SC	0.140	0.009	0.075	1.53 n.s
4.	Mor. SC	0.144	0.004	0.081	1.36 n.s
5.	Int. SC	0.145	0.0009	-0.037	0.35 ns
6.	Phy. SC	0.146	0.0005	0.028	0.18 ns.

Multiple R= 0.382 ** *Significant at .01 level.*
R Square = 0.146

Table 5.14 reveals that sub null Hypotheses No. 12 is rejected, in the case of boys, as the obtained F-value for LOC(20.72>.01) is significant at .01 level. This indicates that LOC (internality dimension) has a significant contribution in the prediction of OI, for boys.

Table 5.14 also shows that the sub null Hypothesis No.7 is retained in the case of boys, because the dimensions of self-concept i.e. Edu. SC (2.78<.05); Soc. SC (1.53<.05); Mor. SC (1.36<.05); Int. SC (0.35<.05); Phy. SC (0.18<.05) have no significant contribution in the prediction of OI, for boys.

The final multiple correlation with the criterion (Goal Selection) is R = 0.479. This multiple correlation accounted for 22.9% of the variance in the prediction of GS for boys. Locus of control accounted for 17.6% of the variance. Social self-concept and Edu. SC accounted for 3.2%and 1.3% of the variance respectively. Another three dimensions of self-concept. i.e. Mor. SC, Phy. SC and Tem. SC added total .75% of the variance. The variable Int. SC did not enter into the equation, because the tolerance level was in sufficient of further computation and as a result the regression was stopped.

Table 5.15
Multiple Regression Analysis Predicting Goal Selection from Dimensions of Self-concept and Locus of Control for Boys

(N = 316).

Sl. No.	*Independent Variables*	*Dependent Variable: Goal Selection (Dimention of Competence Scale)* R^2	*RSQ*	*Beta*	*F-value*
1.	LOC	0.176	0.176	-0.331	37.12**
2.	Soc. SC	0.209	0.032	0.120	4.24*
3.	Edu. SC	0.221	0.127	0.093	2.39 n.s
4.	Mor. SC	0.227	0.005	0.081	1.58 n.s
5.	Phy. SC	0.228	0.001	0.058	0.79 n.s
6.	Tem. SC	0.229	0.001	0.001	0.43 n.s.

Multiple R = 0.479   ** *Significant at .01 level.*
R Square = 0.229   **Significant at .05 level.*

Results presented in Table 5.15 reveals that the sub null Hypothesis No. 13 is rejected in the case of boys as the obtained F-value for LOC (37.12>.01) is significant at .01 level. This indicates that LOC has a significant contribution in the prediction of GS, for boys.

Table 5.15 also shows that the sub null Hypothesis No. 8 is very slightly rejected in the case of boys as the F-value for one of the dimension of self-concept, i.e. Soc. SC (4.24>.05)is significant at .05 level. It means. Soc. SC has a significant contribution in the prediction of GS. While another four dimensions of self-concept), i.e. Edu. SC (2.39<.05); Mor. SC (1.58<.05); Phy. SC (0.79<.05); Tem SC (0.43<.05) are not statistically significant. Therefore. These four variables have no significant contribution in the prediction of GS, for boys.

The final multiple correlation with criterion (planning) is R =0.411. This multiple correlation accounted for 16.8% of the variance with planning. Physical self-concept accounted for 12.2% of the variance. Locus of control accounted for 4..1% of the variance. Social Self-concept, Edu. SC, Tem. SC Int. SC accounted for total .087% of the variance. Physical self-concept did not enter into the equation, because the tolerance level was insufficient for the further computation, and as a result, regression was stopped.

Table 5.16

Multiple Regression Analysis Predicting Planning from Dimensions of Self-concept and Locus of Control for Boys

(N = 316)

Sl. No.	*Independent Variables*	*Dependent Variable: Planning (Dimention of Competence Scale)*			
		R^2	*RSQ*	*Beta*	*F-value*
1.	Phy. SC	0.122	0.122	0.251	14.61**
2.	Loc. SC	0.163	0.041	-0.213	14.33**
3.	Soc. SC	0.167	0.004	0.066	1.25 n.s
4.	Edu. SC	0.168	0.0004	-0.033	0.26 n.s
5.	Tem.. SC	0.168	0.0005	0.026	0.16 n.s
6.	Int. SC	0.168	0.0002	0.015	0.06 n.s.

Multiple R = 0.411 ** *Significant at .01 level.*
R Square = 0.168

Table 5.16 reveals that the sub null Hypothesis No. 14 is rejected in the case of boys, as the obtained F-value for LOC (14.33>.01) is significant at .01 level. This indicates that LOC has a significant contribution in the prediction of planning, for boys.

Table 5.16 also shows that the sub null Hypothesis No. 9 is very partially rejected, in the case of boys, as the obtained F-value for one of the dimension of self-concept., i.e. Phy. SC (14.33 >.01) is significant at .01 level. It means Phy. SC has a significant contribution in the prediction of plannning for boys. While another four dimensions of self-concept i.e. Soc. SC (1.25<.05); Edu. DC (0.26<.05); Tem. SC (.016<.05); Int. SC (0.06<.05) are not statistically significant. Therefore these four variables have no significant contribution in the prediction of planning, for boys.

Table 5.17
Multiple Regression Analysis Predicting Problem Solving from Dimensions of Self-concept and Locus of Control for Boys *(N = 316)*

Sl. No.	Independent Variables	*Dependent Variable: Problem Solving (Dimention of Competence Scale)* R^2	RSQ	Beta	F-value
1.	LOC	0.106	0.106	-0.226	15.76**
2.	Phy. SC	0.142	0.037	0.139	4.22**
3.	Mor. SC	0.152	0.009	0.075	1.19 n.s
4.	Edu. SC	0.156	0.004	0.067	1.07 n.s.
5.	Int. SC	0.158	0.002	0.058	0.86 n.s
6.	Tem. SC	0.159	0.001	-0.051	0.63 n.s
7.	Soc. SC	0.159	0.0005	0.026	0.18 n.s.

Multiple R = 0.399 ** Significant at .01 level.
R Square = 0.159 * Significant at .05 level.

The final multiple correlation with the criterion (problem solving) is R = 0.399. This multiple correlation accounted for 15.9% of the variance in the prediction of problem solving. Locus of control accounted for 10.6% of the variance with the PS. Physical self-concept accounted for 3.6% of the variance. The remaining five dimensions of self-concept, i.e. Mor. SC, Edu. SC, Int. SC, Tem. SC and Soc. SC accounted for 1.6% of the variance.

Results presented in Table 5.17 reveals that the sub null Hypothesis No. 15 is rejected in the case of boys, because the obtained F-value for LOC (15.76>.01) is significant at .01 level. This indicates that the LOC has a significant contribution in the prediction of problem solving.

Table 5.17 also shows that the null Hypothesis No. 10 is slightly rejected, because out of six, one dimension of self-concept i.e. Phy. SC. (4.22>.05) is significantly contributes to PS. While the F-values for remaining five dimensions of self-concept, i.e. Mor. SC (1.19<.05); Edu. SC (1.07 <.05); Int. SC (.86<.05); Temp SC (0.63<.05); and Soc. SC (0.18<.05) are not statistically significant.

Therefore these five variables have no significant contribution in the prediction of PS, for boys.

Table 5.18
Multiple Regression Analysis Predicting Competencies of Career Maturity (Total) from Dimensions of Self-concept and Locus of Control for boys *(N=316)*

Sl. No.	*Independent Variables*	*Dependent Variable: Competencies of Career Maturity (Total)*			
		R^2	*RSQ*	*Beta*	*F-value*
1.	LOC	0.228	0.228	-0.371	51.55**
2.	Soc. SC	0.296	0.021	0.139	6.25**
3.	Phy. SC	0.275	0.046	0.139	5.09*
4.	Mor. SC	0.304	0.008	0.111	3.52 n.s.
5.	Tem. SC	0.305	0.0009	0.050	0.64 n.s
6.	Edu. SC	0.306	0.001	-0.036	0.41 n.s
7.	Int. SC	0.307	0.0007	-0.032	0.31 n.s.

Multiple R = 0.554 — ** *Significant at .01 level.*
R Square = 0.307 — * *Significant at .05 level.*

Table 5.18 shows that the final multiple correlation with the criterion (competencies of career maturity) is R = 0.554.

This multiple correlation accounted for 30.7% of the variance in the prediction of competencies of career maturity. Locus of control accounted for 22.8% of the variance in the prediction of competencies of career maturity. Social self-concept and Phy. SC accounted for 2.1% and 4.6% of the variance respectively. Remaining four dimensions of self-concept i.e. Mor., Tem., Edu. and Int. accounted for another additional 1.2% of the variance in the prediction of competencies of career maturity among boys.

Table 5.18 reveals that the major null Hypothesis No. VI is rejected in the case of boys, as the obtained F-value for LOC (51.55>.01) is significant. It means that locus of control has a significant contribution in the prediction of comp. of CM, among boys.

Table 5.18 also shows that major null Hypothesis No. IV is partially rejected, because the two dimensions of self-concept i.e. Soc. (6.25>.01) and Phy. (5.09>.05) have significant contribution in the prediction of comp. of CM. While remaining four dimensions of self-concept i.e. Mor (3.52<.05); Tem. (.64<.05); Edu. (.41<.05) and Int. (.19 <.05) have no significant contribution in the prediction of comp. Of CM for boys.

Results presented in Table 5.19 reveals that the major null Hypothesis No 1 is retained in the case of boys, because self-concept has no significant contribution in the prediction of attitudes towards career maturity (.002%). Major null Hypothesis No. II is rejected in the case of boys, because self-concept has a significant contribution in the prediction of total competencies of career maturity (17.01%).

Table 5.19 reveals that the sub null Hypothesis Nos. 1, 2, 3, 4, & 5 are rejected in the case of boys, because self-concept has a significant contribution in the prediction of SA (21.6%>.01); OI (8.29%>.01); GS (11.92%>.01); planning (9.96%>.01) and problem solving (9.93%>.01)

The final multiple correlation with the criterion (attitudes towards career maturity)' is R = 0.381. This multiple correlation accounted for 14.5% of the variance in the prediction of attitudes towards career maturity, among girls. Moral self-concept accounted for 9.9% of the variance. LOC accounted for 2.6% of the variance. Another four dimensions of self-concept i.e., Int., Phy., Soc., Tem., added another additional 2.01% of the variance with attitudes towards career maturity. Educational self-concept did not enter into the equation, because the tolerance level was insufficient for further computation and as a result the regression was stopped.

Table 5.19
Predicting Attitudes Towards Career Maturity, Dimension of Competence Scale of Career Maturity and Total Competencies of Career Maturity from Self-Concept for Boys

(N=316)

Independent Variable	*Dependent Variable :*		*Attitude Scale of Career Maturity, Competence Scale of Career Maturity and Its Dimensions*											
	Attitude Scale of Career Maturity		*Competence Scale and Its Dimensions*											
			SA		*OI*		*GS*		*Plan*		*PS*		*Total*	
	r	R^2	r	R^2	r	R^2	r	R^2	r	R^2	r	R^2	r	R^2
Self-Concept (total)	0.0474	0.0022	0.2161**	0.0466	0.2879**	0.0829	0.3453**	0.1192	0.3156	0.0996	0.3151**	0.0993	0.4125**	0.1702

SA = Self - Appraisal
QI = Occupational Information
GS = Goal Selection
Plann = Planning
PS = Problem Solving
** *Significant at .01 level*

Among Girls

Table 5.20 :
Multiple Regression Analysis Predicting Attitudes Towards Career Maturity from Dimensions of Self-Concept and Locus of Control for Girls *(N=266)*

Sl. No.	Independent Variables	Dependent Variable: Attitudes Towards Career Maturity			
		R^2	RSQ	Beta	F-value
1.	Mor. SC	0.099	0.99	0.107	2.53 n.s.
2.	Int.. SC	0.137	0.011	0.102	1.78 n.s.
3.	LOC	0.125	0.026	-0.118	1.71 n.s
4.	Phy. SC	0.143	0.006	0.088	1.45 n.s.
5.	Soc. SC	0.145	0.002	0.050	0.57 n.s
6.	Tem. SC	0.145	0.0005	0.030	0.16 n.s

Multiple R = 0.381
R Square = 0.145

Table 5.20 reveals that the major null Hypothesis No. V is retained in the case of girls, as the obtained F - value (2.53 <.05) is not significant. This indicates that LOC (internality dimension) has no significant contribution in the prediction of attitudes towards career maturity, for girls.

Table 5.20 also shows that the major null Hypothesis No. III is also retained, in the case of girls, as the yielded F-Values for Int. SC (1.78<.05); Mor. SC (1.71 <.05); Phy. SC (1.45<.05); Soc. SC (0.57<.05); Tem. SC (0.16 <.05) are not statistically significant. It means that these variables have no significant contribution in the prediction of attitudes towards career maturity, for girls.

The final multiple correlation with the criterion (self-appraisal) is 0.368. This multiple correlation accounted 13.5% of the variance in the prediction of self-appraisal. Educational self-concept accounted for 7.5% of the variance. Social self-concept accounted for 3.9% of the variance. Remaining four dimensions of self-concept, i.e. Phy., Tem., Mor., Int. added another additional 1.93% of the variance. Locus of control accounted for .2% of the variance in the prediction of self-appraisal, among girls.

Table 5.21
Multiple Regression Analysis Predicting Self-Appraisal From Dimensions of Self-Concept and Locus of Control for Girls *(N=266)*

Sl.	*Independent*	*Dependent Variable: Self-Appraisal (Dimention of Competence Scale)*			
No.	*Variables*	R^2	*RSQ*	*Beta*	*F-value*
1.	Soc. SC	0.114	0.114	0.150	4.87*
2.	Edu. SC	0.075	0.075	0.148	4.69*
3.	Phy. SC	0.131	0.017	0.116	2.49 n.s
4.	LOC	0.134	0.002	-0.045	0.35 n.s.
5.	Tem. SC	0.135	0.001	0.141	0.28 n.s
6.	Mor. SC	0.135	0.0001	0.022	0.07 n.s.
7.	Int. SC	0.135	0.0001	-0.018	0.05 n.s

Multiple R = 0.368
R Square = 0.135 * *Significant at .05 level.*

Table 5.21 reveals that the sub null Hypothesis No. II is retained in the case of girls, as the obtained F-value for LOC (0.35 <.05) is not significant. It means that LOC has no significant contribution in the prediction of SA, among girls.

Table 5.21 reveals that the sub null Hypothesis No. 16 is partially rejected, in the case of girls, because the two dimensions of SC, i.e. Edu. (4.69>.05); and Soc. (4.87>.05) have significant contribution in the prediction of SA. While another four dimensions of SC, i.e. Phy. (2.49 <.05); Tem. (0.28 <.05); Mor. (0.07 <.05); Int. (0.05 <.05) have no significant contribution in the prediction of SA, in the case of girls.

Table 5.22 reveals that the final multiple correlation with the criterion (occupational information) is R=0.425. This multiple correlation accounted for 18% of the

Table 5.22
Multiple Regression Analysis Predicting Occupational Information from Dimensions of Self-concept and Locus of Control for Girls *(N = 266)*

Sl. No.	Independent Variables	*Dependent Variable: Occupational Information (Dimension of Competence Scale)* R^2	RSQ	Beta	F-value
1.	Edu. SC	0.119	0.119	0.225	11.29**
2.	Soc. SC	0.152	0.034	0.142	4.60*
3.	Int. SC	0.177	0.008	-0.138	3.33 n.s
4.	Phy. SC	0.169	0.005	0.101	1.99 n.s.
5.	LOC	0.164	0.011	-0.102	1.90 n.s
6.	Mor. SC	0.180	0.004	0.086	1.05 n.s
7.	Tem. SC	0.180	0.0001	0.014	1.04 n.s.

Multiple R = 0.425 ** Significant at .01 level.
R Square = 0.180 * Significant at 05 level

of the variance in the prediction of OI in girls. Educational Self-concept and Soc. SC accounted for 11.9% and 3.4 % of the variance respectively. Remaining four dimensions of self-concept i.e. Phy., Int., Mor., Tem. added another additional 1.71 % of the variance. Locus of control accounted for 1.1% of the variance in the prediction of OI. for girls.

Table 5.22 reveals that the sub null Hypothesis No. 12 is retained in the case of girls, as the obtained F-value for LOC (1.90 <.05) is not significant. It means LOC has no contribution in the prediction of OI, among girls.

Table 5.22 also shows that the sub null Hypothesis No.7 is partially rejected in the case of girls because the two dimensions of self-concept. i.e. Edu. (11.29>.01), Soc. (4.60>.05) have a significant contribution in the prediction of OI. While remaining four dimensions of self-concept, i.e. Phy. (1.99 <.05); Int. (3.33 <.05); Mor. (1.05<.05); and Tem. (0.04<.05) have no significant contribution in the prediction of OI, for girls.

Table 5.23
Multiple Regression Analysis Predicting Goal Selection from the Dimensions of Self-concept and Locus of Control for Girls (N = 266)

Sl. No.	*Independent Variables*	*Dependent Variable: Goal Selection (Dimension of Competence Scale)*			
		R^2	*RSQ*	*Beta*	*F-value*
1.	Mor. SC	0.146	0.146	0.144	3.01 n.s.
2.	Tern. SC	0.185	0.012	0.105	1.99 n.s.
3.	LOC. SC	0.172	0.026	-0.101	1.93 n.s.
4.	Soc. SC	0.191	0.006	0.086	1.71 n.s.
5.	Int. SC	0.196	0.005	0.084	1.27 n.s.
6.	Edu. SC	0.198	0.001	0.044	0.45 n.s.
7.	Phy. SC	0.198	0.0005	0.029	0.17 n.s.

Multiple R = 0.445
R Square = 0.198

The final multiple correlation with the criterion (Goal Selection) is R = 0.445. This multiple correlation accounted for 19.8% of the variance in the prediction of GS for girls. Moral self-concept accounted for 14.6% of the variance. LOC accounted for 2.6 % of the variance. Remaining five dimensions of self-concept, i.e. Tern., Soc., Int., Edu., Phy., added another additional 2.65% of the variance in the prediction of GS, among girls.

Table 5.23 reveals that the sub null Hypothesis No. 13 is retained in the case of girls, as the obtained F-value for LOC (1.93 <.05) is not significant. It means that LOC has no significant contribution in the prediction of GS, among girls.

Table 5.23 also shows that the sub null Hypothesis No. 8 is also retained as the F-value for all the dimensions of self-concept, i.e. Mor. (3.01 <.05); Tem. (1.99 <.05); Soc. (1.71 <.05); Int. (1.27<.05) are not significant. This indicates that these dimensions self-concept have no significant contribution in the prediction of goal selection, among girls.

Table 5.24
Multiple Regression Analysis Predicting Planning from Dimensions of Self-concept and Locus of Control for Girls (N = 266)

Sl. No.	Independent Variables	Dependent Variable: Planning (Dimension of Competence Scale)			
		R^2	*RSQ*	*Beta*	*F-value*
1.	Mar. SC	0.140	0.140	0.124	2.23 n.s.
2.	In. SC	0.178	0.013	0.104	1.95 n.s.
3.	Tem. SC	0.165	0.025	0.099	1.79 n.s.
4.	Phy. SC	0.184	0.006	0.075	1.12 n.s.
5.	Soc. SC	0.189	0.005	0.066	1.01 n.s
6.	Edu. SC	0.192	0.004,	0.063	1.89 n.s
7.	LOC	0.194	0.002	-0.063	0.74 n.s.

Multiple R = 0.441
R Square = 0.194

Table 5.24 shows that the final multiple correlation with the criterion (Planning) is R = 0.441. This multiple correlation accounted for 19.4% of the variance in the prediction of planning. Moral self-concept accounted for 14% of the variance. Temperamental Self-concept and Int. SC accounted for 2.5% and 1.3% of the variance respectively. The remaining three dimensions of self-concept, i.e. Phy., Soc. and Edu. added another additional 1.4% of the variance. Locus of control accounted for .2% of the variance in the prediction of planning, among girls.

Table 5.25 reveals that the sub null Hypothesis No. 14 is retained in the case of girls, as the obtained F-value for LOC (0.74 <.05) is not significant. It means that LOC has no significant contribution in the prediction of planning, for girls.

Table 5.25 also shows that the sub null Hypothesis No. 9 is also retained, in the case of girls, as the obtained F-values for all the dimensions of self-concept, i.e. Mor. (2.23 <.05); Tem. (1.79 <.05); Int. (1.95 <.05);

Phy, (1.12 <.05); Soc. (1.01 <.05) and Edu. (0.89<.05) are not significant. This indicates that all these dimensions of self-concept have no significant contribution in the prediction of planning, among girls.

Table 5.25

Multiple Regression Analysis Predicting Problem Solving from Dimension of Self-concept and Locus of Control for Girls

Sl. No.	*Independent Variables*	*Dependent Variable: Problem Solving (Dimension of Competence Scale)*			
		R^2	*RSQ*	*Beta*	*F-value*
1.	Mor.SC	0.244	0.244	0.223	8.74**
2.	Tem.SC	0.290	0.046	0.164	5.79**.
3.	LOC	0.308	0.018	-0.123	3.37 n.s.
4.	Soc. SC	0.317	0.009	0.106	3.11 n.s.
5.	Phy.SC	0.320	0.003	0.063	0.94 n.s
6.	Int. SC	0.322	0.002	0.059	0.75 n.s
7.	Edu. SC	0.322	0.00006	-0.009	0.02 n.s.

Multiple R = 0.568 **Significant at .01 level
R Square = 0.322

The final multiple correlation with the criterion (problem solving) is R=0.568. This multiple correlation accounted for 32.2% of the variance in the prediction of PS in the case of girls. Moral self-concept and Tem. SC accounted for 24.4% and 4.6% of the variance respectively. Remaining four dimensions of self-concept, i.e. Soc., Phy., Int. and Edu. added another additional 1.36 of the variance. Locus of control accounted for 1.8% of the variance in the prediction of PS, among girls.

Table 5.25 reveals that the sub nul Hypothesis No. 15 is retained in the case of girls, as the obtained F-value for LOC (3.37 <.05) is not significant. It means LOC has no significant contribution in the prediction of PS, among girls.

Table 5.25 reveals that the sub null Hypothesis No.

10 is partially rejected as the F-value for two dimensions of self-concept, i.e. Mor. (8.74>.01) and Tem. (5.29> .05) are significant at .01 and .05 level of significance respectively. It means that these two dimensions have significant contribution in the prediction of PS, for girls. While remaining four diinensions of self-concept, i.e. Soc. SC (3.11<.05); Phy. (0.94 <.05); Int. (0.75 <05); Edu., (0.02 <.05) are not statistically significant. This indicates that these variables have no significant contribution in the prediction of PS, among girls.

Table 5.26

Multiple Regression Analysis Predicting Competencies of Career maturity (Total) from dimensions of Self-concept and Locus of Control for Girls (N = 266)

Sl. No.	*Independent Variables*	*Dependent Variable: Competencies of Career Maturity (Total)*			
		R^2	*RSQ*	*Beta*	*F-value*
1.	Soc.SC	0.310	0.021	0.139	6.53**
2.	Edu. SC	0.341	0.0008	0.050	4.84*
3.	Mor.SC	0.246	0.228	-0.371	4.59*
4.	LOC	0.290	0.046	0.139	3.21 n.s.
5.	Tem.SC	.0.349	0.001	-0.036	3.01 n.s
6.	Phy. SC	0.329	0.008	0.111	2.81 n.s
7.	Int. SC	0.350	0.0006	-0.032	0.19 n.s.

Multiple R = 0.592
R Square = 0.350

**Significant at .01 level
* Significant at .05 level

Table 5.26 shows that final multiple correlation with the criterion competencies of career maturity (Total) is R = 0.592. This multiple correlation accounted for 35% of the variance in the prediction of comp. of CM (Total). Moral self-concept accounted for 24.6% of the variance. Social self-concept accounted for 2.3% of the variance. Physical self-concept and Edu. SC accounted for 1.6% and 1.2% of the variance respectively. Remaining two dimensions of self-concept, i.e. Tem., and Int. accounted for another additional. 85% of the variance. Locus of control accounted for 4.4% of the variance in the prediction of comp. of CM (total) among girls.

Table 5.26 reveals that the major null Hypothesis No. VI is retained in the case of girls, as the obtained F-value for LOC (3.21 <.05) is not significant. It means that LOC has no significant contribution in the prediction of comp. of CM (total) among girls.

Table 5.26 also depicts that the major null Hypothesis No. IV is partially rejected, because the three dimensions of self-concept, i.e. Soc. (6.53>.01); Edu. (4.84>.05); Mor. (4.59>.05) have significant contribution in the prediction of comp. of CM (total). On the other hand remaining three dimensions of self-concept, i.e. Phy. (2.81<.05); Tem. (3.01<.05); Int. (0.19<.05) have no significant contribution in the prediction of comp. of CM (total) among girls.

Results presented in Table 5.27 reveals that the major null Hypothesis Nos. I & II are rejected in the case of girls, because self-concept has a significant contribution in the prediction of attitudes towards career maturity (13.65%) and total competencies of career maturity (32.44 %), which are significant at .01 and .05 level respectively.

Table 5.27 reveals that the sub null Hypothesis Nos. 1,2, 3,4 & 5 are rejected in the case of girls, because self-concept has a significant contribution in the prediction of SA (11.3%); OI (11.67%); GS (18.46); Planning (18.62%) and PS (29.29%). All the values are significant at .01 level.

Table 5.28 reveals that the relationship of dimensions of self-concept such as Phy., Soc., Tem., Int. and total SC with attitudes towards career maturity are positive and significant at .01 level. And the relationship between Tem. SC and attitudes toward CM is positive and significant at .05 level. Whereas, the relationship of Edu. SC and Mor. SC to attitudes towards career maturity is positive but not significant.

Table 5.27

Predicting Attitudes Towards Career Maturity, Dimensions of Competence Scale of Career Maturity and Total Competencies of Career Maturity from Self-Concept for Girls

(N=266)

Independent Variable	*Dependent Variable :* *Attitude Scale of Career Maturity*		*Attitude scale of career maturity, competence Scale of Career Maturity and Its Dimensions* — *Competence Scale and Its Dimensions*											
			SA		*OI*		*GS*		*Plann*		*PS*		*Total*	
	r	R^2	*r*	R^2	*r*	R^2	*r*	R^2	*r*	R^2	*r*	R^2	*r*	R^2
Self-Concept (total)	0.3695**	0.1365	0.3362**	0.1130	0.3416**	0.1167	0.4297**	0.1846	0.4315*	0.1862	0.5412**	0.2929	0.5696*	0.3244

SA = Self - Appraisal
OI = Occupational Information
GS = Goal Selection
Plann = Planning
PS = Problem Solving
** *Significant at .05 level*

Table 5.28

Co-efficient Correlation between Self-concept Scores and Locus of Control with Attitudes Towards Career Maturity and Dimensions of Competence Scale of Career Maturity

N=582.

		Dependent Variable						
Sl. No.	*Independent Variables*	*Attitude Towards CM*	*Competence Scale*					
			SA	*OI*	*GS*	*Plann*	*PS*	*Total*
1.	Phy. SC	0.164**	0.182**	0.226**	0.268**	0.322**	0.298**	0.359**
2.	Soc. SC	0.136**	0.251**	0.237**	0.278**	0.249**	0.272**	0.356**
3.	Tem.SC	0.111*	0.166**	0.254**	0.299**	0.263**	0.315**	0.352**
4.	Edu. SC	0.099	0.078	0.141**	0.226**	0.215**	0.255**	0.248**
5.	Mor. SC	0.096	0.232**	0.274**	0.259**	0.201**	0.239**	0.327**
6.	Int. SC	0.155**	0.146**	0.178**	0.219**	0.265**	0.282**	0.297**
7.	Total SC	0.175**	0.256**	0.306**	0.365**	0.355**	0.389**	0.458**
8.	LOC	-0.233**	-0.311**	-0.308**	-0.383**	-0.336**	-0.413**	-0.478**

** *Significant at .01 level*

* *Significant at .05 level*

Table 5.28 also shows that the relationship of different dimensions of self-concept with the different dimensions of competence scale of career maturity and total scores on competence scale is positive and significant at .01 level.

Table 5.28 depicts that the relationship of LOC with attitudes towards career maturity, different dimensions of competence scale and total score on competence scale is negative and significant at .01 level.

Results presented in Table 5.28 reveals that the major null Hypothesis Nos. IX and XI, and sub null Hypothesis Nos. 21, 22, 23, 24, and 25 are rejected, because self-concept is significantly related with attitudes towards career maturity (.175>.01); different dimensions of competencies of career maturity, i.e. SA (.256) .01; OI (.306>.01); GS (.365>.01); plan. (.355>.01); PS (.389>.01) and total competencies of career maturity (.458>.01).

Table 5.28 also reveals that the major null Hypothesis Nos. XIII and XIV, and sub null Hypothesis Nos. 31, 32, 33, 34 and 35 are rejected, because LOC is significantly negatively related with attitudes towards career maturity (-.233>.01), different dimensions of competence scale of career maturity, i.e. SA (-.311>.01); OI (-.308>.01); GS (-.383>.01) and total competencies (-.478>.01) of career maturity. This indicates that internality is significantly related with career maturity.

Table 5.28 reveals that the major null Hypothesis No. X is partially retained because an attitude towards career maturity is not significantly related with Edu. SC (.099 <.05) and Mor. SC (.096 <.05). While there is significant relationship between remaining four dimensions of self-concept such as Phy., Tem. and Int. SC with attitudes towards career maturity.

Results presented in Table 5.28 also depicts that the sub nuli Hypothesis Nos. 27, 28, 29 and 30 are rejected, because there is significant relationship between

Table 5.29

Co-efficient correlation between self-concept scores and Locus of control with attitudes Towards Career Maturity and Dimensions of Competence Scale of Career Maturity of Boys

(N = 316)

Sl. No.	*Independent Variables*	*Dependent Variable*						
		Attitude Towards CM	*Competence Scale*					
			SA	*OI*	*GS*	*Plann*	*PS*	*Total*
1.	Phy. SC	0.094	0.151*	0.213**	0.272**	0.349**	0.285**	0.356**
2.	Soc.SC	0.068	0.220**	0.201	0.264**	0.214**	0.181**	0.308**
3.	Tem.SC	-0.019	0.138	0.241**	0.292**	0.229**	0.264**	0.319**
4.	Edu. SC	0.003	0.032	0.143*	0.198**	0.170**	0.219**	0.206**
5.	Mor. SC	0.029	0.221**	0.237**	0.271**	0.171**	0.239**	0.312**
6.	Int. SC	0.068	0.075	0.145*	0.149*	0.195**	0.136**	0.192**
7.	Total SC	0.047	0.216**	0.288**	0.345**	0.316**	0.315**	0.413**
8.	LOC	-0.165*	-0.335**	-0.329**	-0.420**	-0.304**	-0.325**	-0.478**

** *Significant at .01 level*

* *Significant at .05 level*

dimensions of self-concept with the dimensions of competence scale of career maturity, i.e. OI, GS, Plann., and PS. While sub null Hypothesis No. 26 is partially retained, because there is no significant 'r' between Edu. SC and SA (.078 <.05). While remaining five dimensions of self-concept are significantly related with SA.

Table 5.29 reveals that the relationship of dimensions of self-concept such as Phy., Soc., Tem., Edu., Mor., Int. and Total Self-concept with attitudes towards career maturity are not significant.

Table 5.29 also shows that the relationship between dimensions of self-concept such as Phy., Soc., Tem., Edu., Int., and total SC with the different dimensions of competence scale of career maturity and total scores on competence scale of career maturity are significant at .01 level, except the 'r' between Phy. SC and SA; Int. SC and OI; and Int. SC and GS, which are significant at .05 level.

Table 5.29 also reveals that the relationship of LOC with attitudes towards career maturity is significant at .05 level. The co-efficient of correlation between locus of control with different dimensions of competence scale and total scores on competence scale is significant at .01 level.

Results presented in Table 5.29 reveals that major null Hypothesis Nos. IX and X are retained in the case of boys, because there is no significant relationship between total SC and Attitudes. Towards CM (.047 <.05); and, there is no significant relationship between dimensions of self-concept such as Phy. (.094 < .05); Soc. (.068<.05); Tem. (-0.019<.05); Edu. (.003<.05); Mor. (0.29<.05) and Int. (.068<.05) with attitudes towards career maturity.

Inspection of Table 5.29 indicates that major null Hypothesis Nos. XI, XII, XIII and XIV are rejected in the case of boys, because there are significant 'r' between Total SC & Comp. of CM (.413>.01); Dimensions of SC such as Phy. (.356>.01); Soc. (.308>.01), Tem. (.319>.01), Edu. (.206>.01), Mor. (.312>.01) and Int. (.192>.01) with competencies of career maturity; LOC and attitudes towards career maturity (-.165>.05) and LOC and comp. of CM (-.478> .01)

Table 5.29 reveals that the sub null Hypothesis Nos. 28, and 29 are rejected in the case of boys, because the 'r' between all the dimensions of self-concept with GS and Plann, are significant. Sub null Hypothesis Nos. 26, 27 and 30 are partially retained in the case of boys, because the co-efficient of correlation between Tem. SC & SA (.138 <.05), Edu. SC & SA (.032<.05), Edu. SC & OI (.143<.05), Int. SC & SA (.075<.05), Int. SC & PS (.136 <.05) are not significant. While there is a significant relationship between remaining dimensions of self-concept and dimensions of competence scale of career maturity.

Table 5.29 depicts that the sub null Hypothesis Nos. 31,32,33,34 & 35 are rejected in the case of boys, because there is a significant relationship between LOC and dimensions of competence scale of career maturity. This indicates that internally is significantly related with dimensions of comp. of career maturity.

Table 5.29 reveals that the relationship of dimensions of self-concept such as Phy., Soc., Tem., Edu., Mor., Int. and Total self-concept with attitudes towards career maturity are significant at .01 level.

Table 5.29 also shows that the co-efficient of correlation between dimensions of self-concept such as Phy., Soc., Tem., EDU., Int. and total Self-concept with the different dimensions of competence scale of career maturity and total scores on competence scale of career maturity are significant at .01 level, except the 'r' between Edu. SC and OI (.154 <.05), which is not significant.

Table 5.29 reveals that the LOC is significantly related with attitudes towards career maturity, different dimensions of competence scale of career mturity and

Table 5.30

Co-efficient Correlation between Self-concept Scores and Locus of Control with Attitudes Towards Career Maturity and Dimensions of Competence Scale of Career Maturity of Girls

(*N* = 266)

Sl. No.	*Independent Variables*	*Dependent Variable*						
		Attitude Towards CM	*Competence Scale*					
			SA	*OI*	*GS*	*Plann*	*PS*	*Total*
1.	Phy. SC	0.282**	0.264**	0.259**	0.289**	0.314**	0.381**	0.414**
2.	Soc.SC	0.229**	0.273**	0.283**	0.289**	0.272**	0.365**	0.406**
3.	Tem.SC	0.315**	0.265**	0.302**	0.382**	0.374**	0.494**	0.497**
4.	Edu. SC	0.301**	0.207**	0.154	0.335**	0.345**	0.405**	0.398**
5.	Mor. SC	0.200**	0.273**	0.345**	0.261**	0.269**	0.287**	0.394**
6.	Int. SC	0.268**	0.231**	0.219**	0.342**	0.339**	0.451**	0.433**
7.	Total SC	0.369**	0.336**	0.342**	0.429**	0.432**	0.541**	0.559**
8.	LOC	-0.304**	-0.246**	-0.284**	-0.339**	-0.318**	-0.426**	-0.441**

** Significant at .01 level

total score on competence scale of career maturity. All the calculated 'r' are significant at .01 level.

Results presented in Table 5.30 reveals that the major null Hypothesis No. IX is rejected in the case of girls, because there is a significant 'r' between total self-concept and attitudes towards career maturity

Major null Hypothesis No. X is also rejected in the case of girls because dimensions of self-concept such as Phy., Soc., Tem., Edu., Mor. and Int. are significantly related with attitudes towards career maturity. All the values of 'r' are significant at .01 level.

Table 5.32 also reveals that the major null Hypothesis Nos. XI and XII are rejected in the case of girls, because the self-concept and its dimensions such as Phy., Soc., Tem., Edu., Mor. and Int. are significantly related with total competencies of career maturity. All the values of 'r' are significant at .01 level.

Results presented in Table 5.30 indicates that the major null Hypothesis Nos. V and VI are rejected in the case of girls, because LOC is significantly related with attitudes towards career maturity and total comp. of CM. Both the values of 'r' are significant at .01 level.

Table 5.30 reveals that the sub null Hypothesis Nos. 26, 28, 29 and 30 are rejected in the case of girls, because dimensions of self-concept such as Phy., Soc., Tem., Edu., Mor., Int. are significantly related with dimensions of competence scale of career maturity, i.e. SA, GS, Plann., and PS. While sub null Hypothesis No. 27 is partially retained in the case of girls, as the Edu. SC is not significantly related with OI (.154 <.05). While remaining dimension of self-concept is significantly related with OI.

Table 5.31

Mean, Standard Deviation and t-Value of Boys and Girls on Career Maturity with df = 580.

Sl. No.	Variables	Boys (N = 316) Mean	SD	Girls (N=266) Mean	SD	t-values
1.	Attitude of Career Maturity	30.51	6.96	31.03	6.31	0.95n.s
2.	Competence Scale of Career Maturity					
i.	SA	8.11	2.38	8.85	1.96	4.08**
ii.	OI	8.69	2.61	9.06	2.12	1.89n.s.
iii.	GS	8.16	2.62	8.79	1.72	3.41**
iv.	Plann	6.82	2.76	7.84	2.59	4.56**
v.	P.S.	5.99	2.15	7.23	2.06	7.07**
vi	Competencies of career Maturity (Total)	37.78	9.08	41.75	7.65	5.65**

** *Significant at .01 level.*

Table 5.31 reveals that the mean scores of attitudes towards career maturity of boys is 30.51; girls 31.03. the calculated 't' value is not significant. Therefore the major null Hypothesis No. XV, that there will be no significant difference between boys and girls is retained.

The mean scores of dimensions of competence scale such as SA, OI, GS, Plann. And PS of boys are 8.11, 8.69, 8.16, 6.82, 5.99 respectively. The mean scores of dimensions of competence scale such as SA, Oil, GS, Plann, and PS of girls are 8.85, 9.06, 8.79, 7.84 and 7.23 respectively. All the calculated t-values except one value, i.e. of OI are significant at .01 level. Therefore the sub null Hypothesis Nos. 36, 38, 39 and 40 are rejected, while null Hypothesis No. 37 is retained.

The mean score of total competencies of career maturity of boys is 37.78. The mean score of total competencies of career maturity of girls is 41.75. the calculated 't' value of total competencies of career maturity is significant at .01 level. Therefore the major null Hypothesis No. XVI is rejected.

SUMMARY OF RESULTS

1. Self- concept has no significant contribution in the prediction of attitudes towards career maturity for boys, but it is a significant predictor for girls and for total sample.
2. Dimension of self-concept such as Phy., Soc., Tem., Edu., Mor., and Int. have no significant contribution in the prediction of attitudes towards career maturity, for both boys and girls (separately) and for total sample.
3. Self-concept has a significant contribution in the prediction of competencies of career maturity for boys, girls and for total sample.
4. In the case of total sample four dimensions of self-concept such as Soc., Phy., Edu., Mor., and Int. have significant contribution in the prediction of competencies of career maturity. In the case of boys, only two dimensions of self concept., i.e. Soc. and Phy. have significant contribution in the Prediction of competencies of career maturity, while in the case of girls, three dimensions of self-concept, i.e. Mor., Soc. and Edu. Have significant contribution in the prediction of competencies of career maturity.
5. Self-concept has a significant contribution in the prediction of dimensions of competence scale of career maturity i.e. SA, OI, GS, Plann., and PS for boys, girls and total sample.
6. In the case of boys and girls separately, two dimensions of self-concept, i.e. Soc and Edu. have significant contribution in the prediction of self-appraisal, while as far as total sample is concerned, three dimensions of self-concept such as Soc., Edu., and Int. predict SA.
7. Dimensions of self-concept such as Phy., Soc., Tem.,

Edu., Mor. and Int. have no contribution in the prediction of OI, for boys, but in the case of girls and for total sample, two dimensions of self-concept, i.e. Edu., and Soc. do predict OI.

8. Only two dimensions of self-concept, i.e. Edu. and soc. Predict Goal selection for total sample. All the dimensions of self-concept have no significant contribution in the prediction of GS in the case of girls, while for boys one dimension of self-concept, i.e. Soc. Predict GS.
9. All the dimensions of self-concept have no contribution in the prediction of planning for girls. While in the case of boys and for total sample, one dimension of self concept, i.e. phy. Predicts planning.
10. Physical self-concept predicts problem solving in the case of boys; Mor. and Tem. SC predicts PS for girls, while in the case of total sample Mor. and Phy. SC contribute significantly in the prediction of problem solving.
11. Locus of control has a significant contribution in the prediction of attitudes towards career maturity for total sample and boys, while for girls it does not.
12. Locus of control has a significant contribution in the prediction of competencies of career maturity for boys only, and not in the case of girls and for total sample.
13. Locus of control is a significant predictor of SA, OI, GS and plann. For boys and for total sample, but not for girls.
14. Lucs of control is a significant predictor of problem solving for total sample, but not for boys and girls separately.
15. Sex is not a significant predictor of attitudes towards career maturity and total competencies of career maturity.
16. Sex is a significant predictor of SA, GS and plann., but not for OI and PS.
17. Self-concept is not significantly related with attitudes towards career maturity in the case of boys, but a significant 'r' is found in the case of girls and total sample.

18. Self-concept is significantly related with total competencies of career maturity for total sample, and for boys and girls separately.
19. All the dimensions of self-concept is not significantly related with attitudes towards career maturity in the case of boys, but a significant 'r' are found in the case of girls. In the case of total sample Edu. and Mor. SC are not significantly related with attitudes towards career maturity.
20. In the case of total sample, all the dimensions of self-concept are significantly related with attitudes towards career maturity, except the non-significant relationship between Edu. SC and self-appraisal. The non-significant 'r' is found between Tem. SC and SA; Edu. SC and SA Int. SC and SA; Edu. SC and OI, in the case of boys , Other dimensions of self-concept are significantly related with dimensions of competence scale of career maturity. For girls, all the dimensions of self-concept are significantly related with dimensions of competence scale of career maturity, except a non-significant relationship between OI and Edu. SC.
21. Locus of control (internality) is significantly related with attitudes towards career maturity, competencies of career maturity (total and dimensions of competence scale of career maturity for total sample and for boys and girls separately.
22. There is no significant difference between boys and girls in relation to attitudes towards career maturity.
23. Girls are more career mature in comparison to boys as far as total competencies of career maturity and its four dimensions, i. e. self-appraisal, goal selection, planning and problem solving are concerned. While, there is no significant difference between boys and girls in relation to occupational information.

DISCUSSION

One of the major goals of appropriate programming

for school going students is to help them in career development. Career maturity has been conceived of as an important index for career development (Super, 1955; Super and Overstreet, 1960; Crites, 1965). The present study was stimulated by the desire to obtain a better understanding of the factors affecting career maturity of students of the Government Schools of Delhi. It is anticipated that the understanding of the factor's contributing to career maturity will help in developing adequate educational and vocational programmes for higher secondary students.

In the review of the related literature, it was found that relationship between sex and career maturity was inconsistent, while locus of control and self-concept tended to be consistent in relation to career maturity. The results of this study support the findings of the literature reviewed.

It was found in the results that self-concept has a significant contribution in the prediction of competencies of career maturity. It was also a significant predictor of attitudes towards career maturity in the case of girls and for total sample, but not for boys. It was also found in the results that there was positive correlation between self concept and attitudes of career maturity. These findings are consistent with the findings of Ronald E. Pound (1978); Brumlow, Sharon, Lorraine (1980); and Anderson Gregory Robert (1983). Positive 'r' was found between self-concept and competencies of career maturity (total).

This might be due to the fact that it was found that those people who are having high self-concept are well adjusted, highly confident, self-assurance, emotionally balanced, socially mature, high achievers and discrepancies between their real and ideal self-concept is very narrow, they estimate their abilities in a realistic way, that's why they are career mature.

A non-significant 'r' between one of the dimension of self-concept, i.e intellectual self-concept and attitudes towards career maturity was found on total sample and for boys (see table Nos. 5.28 & 5.29 respectively). This might due to the fact that the attitudes elicits the feelings, the subjective reactions, the disposition that the individuals has towards making a career choice and entering the world of work. In this context, intelligence has no direct influence on individuals.

As far as boys are concerned, it was found that attitudes towards career maturity are not significantly related with Soc. SC (.068<.05); Phy. SC (.094<.05); Edu. SC (.003<.05); Mor. SC (.029<.05). While in the case of girl's attitudes towards career maturity was significantly related with dimensions of self-concept. The reason for this might be that the India is a male dominated country. Even though many liberation movements have been launched for the upliftment of women's conditions; but the fact is that the girls and boys are treated differently for considerations regarding the nature of sex differences and their implications for entry and adjustment into careers. Since childhood, parents express their wishes infront of their male child that he would become a doctor, engineer, etc., because of it boys take it for granted that they are meant for such professions.

While in the case of girls, at present, with the support of women's welfare organization and the spread of the women's liberation movement, they conceptualizes themselves as equal members of society, which operate to increase feminine self-concept. And because of high self-concept now women are entering more confidently and rapidly into the world of work. So we can conclude that in the case of girls an attainment of career maturity is a process, while in the case of boys it is an event, because of the above said reason.

Locus of control was found to have negative and statistically significant relationship to the criterion, i.e. attitudes towards career maturity. The higher the career maturity of student, lower the scores on locus of control, which indicates that those students who are internal will be more career mature. This finding supports that of other researches (If enwanta, Samuel Sunday Mpama, 1979; Dwyer, Kevin, Michael, 1981; Levie Tycho, 1981; Dood, Betty May, 1983).

It was also found that locus of control was a significant predictor of competence scale of career maturity (total) and its dimension, and also significantly related with it. These findings of this study were consistent with the finding of a study conducted by Grossman, Betty, Jane (1979).

Super (1983) has suggested a five-stage model for assessing career maturity (Planfulness, exploration, information, decision making and reality orientation). The first component of stage 1, he lebelled 'autonomy'. Super stated that planning can take place if people believe that they have some control over their careers, often called locus of control, Internally is related with good planning. It was found that internality oriented individuals take less time and make good planning in solving problems. Planning is an important aspect of career maturity also. That's why there was a significant 'r' between career maturity and locus of control (internality).

The predictor variable of sex was not statistically significant in relation to attitudes towards career maturity. There was no statistically significant difference between male and female students in attitudes towards career maturity. The findings of this study are consistent with the findings of Nimkuntod, Parnarai (1978); Seik Daniel, Russell (1978); Carter Arthur Wesley (1982); Keefer, Roxanne Kay (1985).

Results revealed that the mean scores of the girls were significantly higher than the mean scores of the boys on four sub-scales of the competence test of career maturity i.e. self-appraisal, goal selection, planning and problem solving. Similar results were found in other researches also. Butler, Dennis, Arthur (1981) found in a study that females were more career mature than males in the area of career planning, career decision making.

Burkhead, Emily Jane (1981) found that women scored significantly higher than men on the self-appraisal and problem solving. Nwachukwu, Uchenna Ignatisu (1983) found that females were more mature than males in their decision making.

It was also observed that girls were more career mature in comparison to boys in relation to competencies of career maturity (total). This finding supports that of other researches (Seik, Daniel Russell, 1978; Anderson, Gregory Robert, 1983).

It was hypothesized that there would be no significant difference in relation to career maturity of boys and girls. But, it was clear from the results that these hypotheses were partially retained, because girls were more career mature than boys. This might be due to development and spread of female career awareness concerns regarding women's uplift have surfaced in the areas of intervention of government and non-government level. The most illustrious advancement in regards to the issues of girls education and employment have taken place during the United National Decade for Women (1975-1985), and the declaration of the year (1975) as the International Women's Year. The National Policy of Education - 1986, has given due importance to education for women equality. All these efforts put together have added towards their intellectual achievement and career development.

The secondary objective of the present study was to see the application of Super's Self-concept Theory into an Indian context. Super (1963, 1983) bases his theory of career development on the translation of self-concept into vocational terms. The interplay of vocational development and self-concept formation forms the basis of career maturity. According to Super, occupation or career is in part an expression of one's personality and that people search for environment's and vocations that are congruent with their interests and permit them to satisfy and express their personalities. Career choice has been considered as an effort to implement the self-concept in that an individual chooses an occupation congruent with his/her self-concept.

According to Super's vocational life stages the subjects in this study were in the exploratory stage and therefore should have been selecting the occupation through which they would implement their self-concept. Further, because they were in the tentative sub-stage, they should have been giving considerations to their needs, interests, capacities, values, and available opportunities. The vocational task, then is to formulate, ideas regarding an appropriate occupation. Since this requires developing occupational self-concepts that will be of assistance in mediating tentative choice, it seems logical to conclude that the higher the level of self-concept, the higher the level of career-maturity. This was supported by the results of this study.

Implications of the Present Study

Any research effort goes waste, if it does not contribute to the existing knowledge or help the discipline in which it has been made. It must have certain implications and should facilitate the growth of the discipline. The implications of the study are as below:

1. Information regarding the clients' level of career maturity facilities the assessment of the clients readiness to make appropriate career decision.
2. In order to develop an effective career counselling programme to be developed, an assessment must first be made of the adolescent's career maturity. Students with career maturity appropriate for their age will require different kinds of intervention from those needed by students with low career maturity.
3. This study suggests that practitioners in career counseling may wish to consider the locus of control scores of their clients', inorder to design counselling intervention accordingly.
4. A positive relationship between self-concept and

career maturity was found in the present study. Therefore, during career counselling, counsellor must take self-concept of the students into consideration, and help them in improving it, if needed.

5. It seems that inorder to help adolescents in their vocational development, one must understand and help individualism their personality development, because, this in turn will bring an improvement in career maturity.

SUMMARY

The major aims of the study were : (i) to investigate the contribution of self-concept, locus of control and sex in predicting career maturity; (ii) to see how self-concept, locus of control and sex are related to career maturity; (iii) to examine the significant difference between boys and girls in relation to career maturity. The review of the selected literature indicated that the relationship between self-concept and career maturity, and locus of control and career maturity were tended to be consistent, while the relationship between sex and career maturity was inconsistent.

In the present study, data was collected on a total 700 boys and girls of XI class, which were reduced finally to 582, as the incomplete and casually responded sheets were not taken into account. To measure the variables, i.e. self-concept and career maturity, self-concept questionnaire and an Indian adaptation of career maturity inventory were given to the students. Moreover no suitable scale was available for measuring locus of control, hence the researcher made an Indian adaptation of Children's Nowicki-Strickland Locus of Control Scale (1973) and administered among the students.

The multiple regression analysis, Pearsons' product moment correlation and t-test was used to analyze the obtained data. Following results were found in the present study:

1. Self-concept has no significant contribution in the

prediction of attitudes towards career maturity for boys, but it is a significant predictor for girls and for total sample.

2. Dimensions of self-concept such as Phy., Soc., Tem., Edu., Mor. and Int. have no significant contribution in the prediction of attitudes towards career maturity, for both boys and girls (separately) and for total sample.
3. Self-concept has a significant contribution in the prediction of competencies of career maturity for boys, girls and for total sample.
4. In the case of total sample, four dimensions of self-concept such as Soc., Phy., Edu., Mor., and Int. have significant contribution in the prediction of competencies of career maturity. In the case of boys, only two dimensions of self-concept, i.e. Soc. and Phy. have significant contribution in the prediction of competencies of carrer maturity, while in the case of girls, three dimensions of self-concept, i.e. Mor., Soc. and Edu. have significant contribution in the prediction of competencies of career maturity.
5. Self-concept has a significant contribution in the prediction of dimensions of competence scale of career maturity, i.e. SA, OI, GS, Plann. and PS for boys, girls and total sample.
6. In the case of boys and girls separately, two dimensions of self-concept, i.e. Soc. and Edu. have significant contribution in the prediction of self-appraisal, while as far as total sample is concerned, three dimensions of self-concept such as Soc., Edu. and Int. predict SA.
7. Dimensions of self-concept such as Phy., Soc., Tern., Edu., Mor. and Int. have no contribution in the prediction of OI, for boys, but in the case of girls and for total sample, two dimensions of self-concept, i.e. Edu. and Soc. do predict OI.
8. Only two dimensions of self-concept, i.e. Edu. and Soc. predict goal selection for total sample. All the dimensions

of self-concept have no significant contribution in the prediction of GS in the case of girls, while for boys one dimension of self-concept, i.e. Soc. predicts GS.

9. All the dimensions of self-concept have no contribution in the prediction of planning for girls. While in the case of boys and for total sample, one dimension of self-concept, i.e. Phy. predicts planning.
10. Physical self-concept predicts problem solving in the case of boys; Mor. and Tern. SC predict PS for girls, while in the case of total sample Mor. and Phy. SC contribute significantly in the prediction of problem solving.
11. Locus of control has a significant contribution in the prediction of attitudes towards career maturity for total sample and boys, while for girls it does not.
12. Locus of control has a significant contribution in the prediction of competencies of career maturity for boys only, and not in the case of girls and for total sample.
13. Locus of control is a significant predictor of SA, OI, GS and plann. for boys and for total sample, but not for girls.
14. Locus of control is a significant predictor of problem solving for total sample, but not for boys and girls separately.
15. Sex is not a significant predictor of attitudes towards career maturity and total competencies of career maturity.
16. Sex is a significant predictor of SA, GS and plann., but not for OI and PS.
17. Self-concept is not significantly related with attitudes towards career maturity in the case of boys, but a significant 'r' is found in the case of girls and total sample.
18. Self-concept is significantly related with total competencies of career maturity for total sample, and for boys and girls separately.
19. All the dimensions of self-concept is not significantly related with attitudes towards career maturity in the case of boys, but a significant 'r' are found in the case of girls.

In the case of total sample edu. and mor. SC are not significantly related with attitudes towards career maturity.

20. In the case of total sample, all the dimensions of self-concept are significantly related with attitudes towards career maturity, except the non-significant relationship between Edu. SC and self-appraisal. The non-significant 'r' is found between tern. SC and SA; Edu. SC and SA; int. SC and SA; Edu. SC and OI, in the case of boys. Other dimensions of self-concept are significantly related with dimensions of competence scale of career maturity. For girls, all the dimensions of self-concept are significantly related with dimensions of competence scale of career maturity, except a non-significant relationship between OI and Edu. SC.
21. Locus of control (internality) is significantly related with attitudes towards career maturity, competencies of career maturity (total) and dimensions of competence scale of career maturity for total sample and for boys and girls separately.
22. There is no significant difference between boys and girls in relation to attitudes towards career maturity.
23. Girls are more career mature in comparison to boys as far as total competencies of career maturity and its four dimensions, i.e. self-appraisal, goal selection, planning and problem solving are concerned. While, there is no significant difference between boys and girls in relation to occupational information.

BIBLIOGRAPHY

Aggarwal, N. (1981) A study of factors related to career maturity of school students. In M.B. Buch (Ed.) (1978-83) *Third Survey of Research in Education*. Baroda. Centre of Advanced Study in Education.

Anderson, G.R. (1983) A study of the Cherokee and white eight-grade student career development: Sex, self-concept and attribution. *Dissertation Abstracts International*, **44 (6)**, 1766-A.

Barbara, A.P. and James, C.H. (1972) Relationship of self-concept and feminine role concept to vocational maturity. *Journal of Counselling Psychology*, **19 (2)**, 436-440.

Bartlett, W.E. (1971) Vocational maturity: Its past, present and future development. *Journal of Vocational Behaviour*, **1**, 217-219.

Bigelow, E.A. (1981) The effect of a consumer education and decision making skill instruction on locus of control orientation and career maturity of high school seniors. *Dissertation Abstracts International*, **42 (6)**, 2461-A.

Booth, J.G. (1986) Factors associated with career maturity in community college students. *Dissertation Abstracts International*, **47 (3)**, 789-A.

Borg, W.R. and Gall, M.D. (1983) *Educational Research: An Introduction*. New York: McGraw Hill Book Company.

Brownfain, J.J. (1965) Stability of the self-concept as a dimension of personality. In D.E. Hamacheki (Ed.) *The self in Growth: Teaching and Learning,* Englewood Cliffs, New Jersey: Prentice Hall.

Brumlow, S.L. (1980) An investigation of self-concepts and career attitude maturity levels of students enrolled in vocational courses in selected comprehensive high schools in the state of Georgia. *Dissertation Abstracts International,* **40 (11),** 5836-A.

Buch, M.B. (Ed.) (1978-83) *Third Survey of Research in Education.* Baroda: Centre of Advanced Study in Education.

Buch, M.B. (Ed.) (1983-88) *Fourth Survey of Research in Education,* Vol. I. Baroda: Centre of Advanced Study in Education.

Burkhead, E.J. (1981) Vocational maturity and physically disabled college students. *Dissertation Abstracts International,* **42 (2),** 546-A.

Butler, D.A. (1981) An examination of the effects of grade level, sex, birth order, grade point average, age and work experience on components of career maturity. *Dissertation Abstracts International,* 3834-A.

Carter-Arther, W. (1982) Career attitude maturity and career related decision making of traditional and non-traditional age college students. *Dissertation Abstracts International,* **42 (10),** 4249-A.

Carter, H.D. (1940) The development of vocational attitudes. *Journal of Consulting Psychology,* **4,** 185-191.

Caston, Roberta and Elizabeth, P. (1983) The relationship of participation in three career programmes and the career maturity of gifted high school students. *Dissertation Abstracts International,* **44 (6),** 1691-A.

Cesarano-Delacruz, C. (1986) The relationship of self-efficacy expectations to vocational maturity in male and female graduate students. *Dissertation Abstracts International,* **47 (2),** 420-21-A.

Chand, H. (1979) *Correlates of Vocational Maturity.* Doctoral Dissertation, Department or Education, Punjab University.

Crane, B.B. (1978) Career maturity, work values and personal characteristics, friends or siblings. *Dissertation Abstracts International,* **38 (11),** 6528-A.

Crites, J.O. (1960) *Vocational Psychology: The study of Vocational Behaviour and Development.* New York: McGraw-Hill Book Co.

Crites, J.O. (1971) *The Maturity of Vocational Attitudes in Adolescence.* Washington, D.C.: American Personnel and Guidance Association.

Cronback, L.J. (1960) *Essentials of Psychological Testing.* New York: Harper and Brothers.

Curry, J.A. (1980) The effects of life planning instruction and career counselling on locus of control orientation and career maturity scores of university compensatory education students. *Dissertation Abstracts International,* **41 (5),** 1968-A.

Dillard, J.M. (1976) Relationship between career maturity and self-concepts of suburban and urban-middle and urban lower class preadolescent black males. *Journal of Vocational Behaviour,* **9,** 311-320.

Donahue, J.M. (1985) The effect of maternal employment on adolescent's career maturity, choice of parental role model and perception of parental power. *Dissertation Abstracts International,* **46 (2),** 377-A.

Doods, B.M. (1983) The relationship of career maturity, locus of control and job ratings for LH students. *Dissertation Abstracts International,* **43 (7),** 2309-A.

Drake, J.W. (1979) The effects of a computer assisted career guidance support system upon the vocational maturity of high school sophomores. *Dissertation Abstracts International,* **39(10),** 5947-A.

Dwyer, K.M. (1981) The effect of decision making and life planning instruction on locus of control orientation, career maturity and self -concept of disad vantaged adults. *Dissertation Abstracts International,* **42 (06),** 2609-A.

Dysinger, W.S. (1950) Maturation and vocational guidance. *Occupations,* **29,** 198-201.

Enderlein, T.E. (1975) Causal patterns related to post high school employment satisfaction. *Journal of Vocational Behaviour,* **7,** 57-80.

Farmer, H.S. et al. (1997) *Diversity and Women's Career Development.* Thousand Oaks, CA: Sage.

Floyd, M.E.S. (1985) The effects of a career guidance programme on the career maturity of ninth grade students. *Dissertation Abstracts International,* **46(5),** 1193-A.

Friedberg, S.A. (1983) The relation of vocational maturity, grade, sex and sex-role orientation. *Dissertation Abstracts International,* **44(1),** 73-A.

Garrett, H.E. (1985) *Statistics in Psychology and Education.* Bombay: Vakils, Febber and Simons Ltd.

Gergely, A.F. (1979) The relationship between vocational attitude maturity, gender and occupational deflection of Georgia ninth grade students. *Dissertation Abstracts International,* **39(12),** 7306-A.

Giammatteo, R.R. (1980) Work values clarification, degree of vocational maturity and congruency between one's self-concept and the stereotype of one's probable occupational choice. *Dissertation Abstracts International,* **41(2),** 536-A.

Grossman, B.J. (1979) The effect of decision making skill instruction on locus of control, career choice competency and occupational information seeking behaviour. *Dissertation Abstracts international,* **40(5),** 2552-A.

Gupta, N. (1989) *Manual for Indian Adaptation of Career Maturity Inventory* (Attitude Scale and Competency Test). Agra: National Psychological Corporation.

Ho, Hua, Kuo (1984) Vocational maturity among orthopaedically impaired and normal students in Taiwan, the Republic of China. *Dissertation Abstracts International,* **45 (5),** 1365-A.

Holland, L. (1973) *Making Vocational Choice: A theory of Careers,* New Jersey: Prentice-Hall.

Huntington, Meath and Stewart, J. (1983) The differential effects of three life career development courses on the self-concept and career maturity of college under class-men. *Dissertation Abstracts International,* **42 (10),** 4300-A.

Ifenwanta, Samuel Sunday Mpama (1979) Locus of control, career maturity and perceived needs for life long education of Nigerian students is the United States. *Dissertation Abstracts International,* **39(9),** 5232-A.

Isralsky, M. (1983) Development of a comprehensive behavioural workshop for career maturity and career-decision making. *Dissertation Abstracts International,* **44(4),** 1029-A.

Kathuria, M. (1974) *An investigation of Some Personality Determinants of Vocational Maturity and Career Indecisiveness.* Doctoral Dissertation, Department of Psychology, Rajasthan University.

Keefer, R.K. (1985) The relationship of self-esteem to the career attitude maturity levels of disadvantaged post-secondary students. *Dissertation Abstracts international,* **45 (12),** 3515-A.

Kenneth, C.W. (1987) Scores on the career maturity inventory and self-confidence. *Psychological Reports* **60,** 690.

Kunnu, FB. (1988) The relationship of ego development and career maturity in Nigerian male and female college students. *Dissertation Abstracts International,* **48(8),** 1988-A.

Lawrence, G. (1977-78) Self-concept meta-dimensions and vocational maturity among black male community college students. *Dissertation Abstracts International,* **38 (7-8),** 3965-A.

Lee, J.C. (1979) Career decision-making patterns of university students as related to career maturity. *Dissertation Abstracts International,* **39(7),** 4061-A.

Linda, D.B. (1990) *Career Choice and Development- Applying; Contemporary Theories to Practice.* San Francisco: Jossey-Bass Publishers.

Lowan, G.L.(1979) The effects of teaching goal setting procedures on the career maturity and classroom performance of business college women differing in locus of control. *Dissertation Abstracts International,* **40 (5),** 2424-A.

Luzzo, D.A. "Gender and Ethnic Differences in the Perception of Barriers to Career Development." *American Counselling Association Conference paper,* Denver, CO, April 1995. (ED 383 978)

Mar-Brennan, C-.D. (1981) The effects of a computer based career guidance system on the development of self-concept and career maturity of community college students, *Dissertation Abstracts International,* **42 (1),** 88-A.

Mause, R. (1980-81) Career maturity of emotionally mal-adjusted high school students. *Vocational Guidance Quarterly,* **29 (1-4),** 213-220.

McCaffrey (1980) A study of career maturity in graduate and undergraduate students. *Dissertation Abstracts International,* **40A (7),** 3784-A.

McNair, D. (1981) A multiple regression analysis using self-concept, parental influence, socio-economic status, degree of certainty, race and sex to predict career maturity, occupational aspirations and occupational expectations. *Dissertation Abstracts International,* **41(8),** 3428-A.

McNamara, L.C. (1975) Twelfth graders'vocational maturity and their subsequent vocational adjustment. *Dissertation Abstracts International,* **36,** 710-A.

Ministry of Human Resource Development. *National Policy on Education-1986. Government of India,* (Department of Education), New Delhi.

Mintzer, R.G. (1976) Vocational maturity and its relationship to intelligence, self-concept, sex-role identification and grade level. *Dissertation Abstracts International,* **37(5),** 2643-A.

Mobley, J.E. (1980) An investigation of the relationship between self-concept, adult vocational maturity, locus of control, work motivation, and reading ability of second career adult males attending a post secondary vocational technical school. *Dissertation Abstracts International,* **41(6),** 7404-A.

Mohy, Y.C. (1980) The vocational maturity of Jamiaican new secondary school students. *Dissertation Abstracts International,* **41(6),** 2575-A.

Nadya, A.F. (1988) The construct of career maturity in the United States and Israel. *Journal of Vocational Behaviour,* **32(1),** 49-591.

Naidoo. A.V. "Career Maturity: A Review of Four Decades of Research," *Bellville,* South Africa: University of the Western Cape, 1998.

Naidoo, A.V.; Bowman, S.L.; and Gerstein, L.H. "Demographic Causality, Work Salience, and the Career Maturity of African-American Students : A Cansal Model." *Journal of Vocational Behaviour* **53,** no. 1, August 1998.

Nimkuntod, P. (1978) Validation and analysis of a measure of career maturity among adolescents of Thailand. *Dissertation Abstracts International,* **38 (12),** 7157-A.

Nowicki, Stephen, Jr. and Strickland, R. Bonnie (1973) A locus of control scale for children. *Journal of Consulting and Clinical Psychology,* **40(1),** 148-154.

Nwachukwu, U.I. (1983) A study of the relationship between levels of career maturity and self-concept in the career development college undergraduate students. *Dissertation Abstracts International,* **44(4),** 992-A.

Okun, N.A. (1984) Handicapped secondary students in two special education programmes: An analysis of self-concept, locus of control and career maturity. *Dissertation Abstracts International,* **44(7),** 2111-A.

Osipow, S.H. (1973) *Theories of Career Development,* New York: Appleton-Century-Crofts.

Parlikar, R.K. (1973) *An Investigation to Study Vocational Maturity of High School Students.* Doctoral Dissertation, Department of Psychology, MSU.

Perez, C.A. (1980) Vocational Maturity and Self-esteem in puertorican youth. *Dissertation Abstracts International,* **41(1),** 110-A.

Pernicono, K.M. (1982) Relationship of sex and complexity to vocational maturity measures and vocational choice. *Dissertation Abstracts International,* **42(7).**

Piper, J.W. (1986) A comparative analysis of career maturity by sex, grade level and curriculum. *Dissertation Abstracts International,* **47(2),** 424-A.

Prince, N.R. (1978) A comparison of eight grade students vocational maturity among four career education approaches. *Dissertation Abstracts International,* **39(4),** 2068-A.

Putnam, B.A.; Hosie, T.W. and Hanien, J.C. (1978) Sex differences in self-concept variables and vocational attitude maturity of adolescents. *Journal of Experimental Education,* **47(1),** 23-27.

Riese, N.J. (1980) Self-concept and vocational maturity of open admissions college students. *Dissertation Abstracts International, 40(11)*, 5838-A.

Robinson, L.T. (1981) The relationship among personality factors. Locus of control and career maturity of education majors at Mississipi valley state University. *Dissertation Abstracts International*, **41(11)**, 4660-A.

Rodebaugh, H.D. (1987) A follow up study of rural adolescents, career maturity, self-concept, personality, anxiety and participation in substance abuse prevention programme. *Digsertation Abstracts International*, **48(1)**, 48-A.

Roe, A. (1957) *Psychology of Occupations.* New York: Harper.

Ronald, E.R (1978) Using self-concept sub-scales in predicting career maturity for race and sex subgroups. *Vocational Guidance Quarterly*, **27 (1-3)**, 61-70.

Saraswat, R.K. (1984) *Manual for Self-Concept Questionnaire.* Agra: National Psychological Corporation.

Saraswat, R.K. and Gaur, J.S. (1981) Approach for the measurement of self-concept: An introduction. *Indian Educational Review*, **16(3)**, 114-119.

Seaward, M.R. (1977) A comparison of the career maturity, self-concept and academic achievement of female cooperative vocational office training students, intensive business training students, and regular business education students in selected high schools in Mississipi. *Dissertation Abstracts-International*, **37**, 4312-A.

Seik, D.R. (1978) A study of the relationship between students voluntary participation in career centres and student career maturity. *Dissertation Abstracts International*, **39 (1)**, 103-A.

Shields, H.C. (1979) The effects of selected career experiences on the career maturity of gifted students. *Dissertation Abstracts International*, **40(6)**, 3263-A.

Smith, G.E. (1987) A study of the career development differences and the relationship of selected variables and career maturity among subpopulation of first year community college business majors. *Dissertation Abstracts International,* **48 (1),** 33-A.

Smith, R. (1981) The study of relationship between career maturity and selected educational, vocational and personal variable. *Dissertation Abstracts International,* **42(1),** 92-A.

Spurlock, L.B. (1984) A study of the relationship of minority to locus of control and selected variables. *Dissertation Abstracts International,* **45 (5),** 1302-A.

Stewart, PJ. (1986) The vocational maturity of adult students. *Dissertation Abstracts International,* **47 (3),** 760-A.

Super, D.E. (1951) Vocational adjustment implementing a self-concept. *Occupations,* **30,** 88-92.

Super, D.E. (1955) The dimensions and measurement of vocational maturity. *Teachers College Record,* **57,** 151-163.

Super, D.E. et al. (1955) *Vocational Development: A Framework for Research.* New York: Bureau of Publications, Teachers College, Columbia University.

Super, D.E., (1957) The psychology of Careers. New York: Harper.

Super, D.E. and Dorothy, D.N. (1984) Work role salience as a determinant of career maturity in high school students. *Journal of Vocational Behaviour,* **25, (1-3),** 30-44.

Super, D.C. and Overstreet, P. (1960) *The Vocational Maturity of Ninth Grade Boys.* New York: Teachers College, Columbia University.

Throndike, R.L. and Hagen, E. (1955) *Measurement and Evaluation in Psychology and Education.* New York: John Wiley and Sons.

Tulsi, RK. (1983) *Differential Effects of Career Guidance Strategies on Vocational Maturity Patterns in to Sex, Intelligence and Need Achievement.* Doctoral Dissertation, Department of Education, Pan. University.

Utairat, W. (1981) Analysis of the EQA scores on the four subscales of self-concept and the vocational maturity scale for school students in Pennsylvania in grade 5th, 8th and 11th. *Dissertation Abstracts International,* **41 (8),** 3551 .

Wylie, R.C. (1974) *The Self-concept.* Lincoln: University of Nebraska Press.

Yankowitz, R.B. (1983) The Structure of Career Maturity in black male and female public high school seniors. *Dissertation Abstracts International,* **43 (8),** 2562-A.

Index